THE
AFRICAN AMERICAN
QUIZ BOOK

for
ALL AMERICANS

✪ Eye-Opening, Interesting and Little-Known Facts of History and Culture, and a Wealth of Information About a Select Group of Individuals Whose Achievements, Heroic Acts, and Creation of Landmark Organizations Have Helped to Make America Great

✪ A Compilation of More Than 350 Non-Trivial Questions and Answers, Designed to Encourage and Stimulate Learning and Critical Thinking, especially for students in Middle Grades, High School and College

✪ An Organized Question and Answer Format That Can Be Easily and Readily Used by Teachers, Families, Churches, Colleges, Sororities and Fraternities, and Community organizations

✪ Includes a Glossary of Terms to Help Maximize Learning, has an Extensive List of References for Further Study and Research, and is also Useful as a Supplementary Text Book

✪ Creative and Original Illustrations are Included to Enhance the Visualization of Persons and Events

THE
AFRICAN AMERICAN
QUIZ BOOK

for
ALL AMERICANS

A Wealth of Knowledge
About History & Culture
Past & Present
(The First of Its Kind)

By
Milton A. Combs, Sr., M.A., M.Div., R.S.T.C.
and
Karyn M. Combs, M.S., & Ed.D.

Illustrated by J. D. Compton

REGENT PRESS
Oakland, CA

ISBN 13: 978-1-58790-121-8
ISBN 10: 1-58790-121-8
Library of Congress Control Number: 2005908732

design: roz abraham

Manufactured in the U.S.A.

Regent Press
6020-A Adeline Street
Oakland, California 94608
www.regentpress.net

TABLE OF CONTENTS

PROLOGUE OF FAMOUS QUOTES

"We hold these truths to be self-evident, that all men are created equal, that they are endowed by their Creator with certain inalienable rights, that among these are Life, Liberty and the pursuit of Happiness."
—2nd Paragraph, U.S.A. Declaration of Independence

"If I have a legacy to leave my people, it is my philosophy of living and serving...I leave you love. Love builds. It is positive and helpful... I leave you hope. Yesterday, our ancestors endured the degradation of slavery, yet they retained their dignity... I leave you thirst for education... Knowledge is the prime need of the hour. —Mary McLeod Bethune, "My Last Will and Testament"

"I have a dream that my four little children will one day live in a nation where they will not be judged by the color of their skin but by the content of their character."
—Martin L. King Jr., 1963 "I Have a Dream" speech

"...You will know the truth, and the truth will make you free." —John 8:32

INTRODUCTION

Purpose and Objectives:

This *African American Quiz Book* is written primarily for the purpose of introducing the reader to some of the little known and unknown historical facts about a select number of persons of African and African American descent and their extraordinary experiences.

Many of these individuals' lives and efforts have done much to enrich and make a positive impact on the life, culture, history and progress of American society from its earliest days to the present, an historical fact that has only become more broadly recognized during the later decades of the 20th century.

For the most part, African American history is not usually taught as an integral and essential part of mainstream American history at any grade level. Yet, as scholars continue to uncover more facts related to this history, it is increasingly apparent that this group of Americans has a long and vital history, one that is closely intertwined with the whole of American history, and one that ought to be regularly included in our education of everyone.

The struggles, perseverance, hardships, strong work ethic, various achievements, patriotism, forgiving spirit, the religious faith and spirituality of African Americans are well documented. When taken together, these attributes of character and values represent a foundation from which many African Americans have been able to survive through the worst oppressive conditions, and yet go on to live worthy lives, and make significant contributions to a wide spectrum of American life and culture.

The main purpose of this Quiz Book is to present brief accounts of African American history and culture within the context of selected topics by means of a question and answer format.

The content is therefore limited in scope, and unique in its approach, compared to a standard history book. And since it is not intended to be a comprehensive and detailed chronological record of African American history, we have included a list of many excellent texts, encyclopedias, books and other scholarly resources that can assist the reader in this regard. Many of these were used as references for the Quiz Book.

Also, this is not a trivia quiz book about African American history because one of its basic objectives is to cite many important and relevant facts integral to understanding American history as a whole, facts which ought to be a part of our common American historical and cultural frame of reference in the 21st century.

Another important objective of the Quiz Book is to

include thought-provoking questions and answers that are designed to encourage and stimulate learning and critical thinking, and a fuller understanding of American history.

In the aftermath of the tragic events of 9/11 and Hurricane Katrina we strongly believe, as educators and citizens, that there is an imperative need for all Americans to build more unity, cooperation and understanding among themselves, and that one of the effective ways this can be done is to provide the reader with some positive facts about the history and culture of African Americans.

We also believe that the information presented in the Quiz Book can help to eliminate some of the various kinds of destructive "isms," misinformation, and lack of information that has plagued and divided us as nation.

Finally, it is hoped that this quiz book can help the reader become more knowledgeable and appreciative of our diverse multicultural American history, even though the focus of this book is primarily on African Americans.

Quiz Book Question and Answer Format:

The question and answer format is used mainly to quickly challenge the reader's knowledge and ability to correctly answer a particular question. This is also a method used to maximize learning, and by doing this, perhaps stimulate further interest and research on the quiz topic questions.

The organization of the book is arranged so that teachers, parents, grandparents and others can readily use it to teach African American history, and to make it an enlightening and enjoyable learning experience as well.

For example, in a school situation, an innovative teacher might assign particular questions to an individual student, a group of students or to an entire class in order to facilitate, and add competition to the learning process. Then, those responding with the correct answers would be given a certain number of predetermined points, letter grade or some other kind of reward.

Similarly, parents might use the quiz book for an interactive family fun activity as a means of teaching and learning about African American history and culture in the context of the home.

Sunday school teachers might use it to supplement their teaching materials as they find it a relevant reference, especially for those organizing various kinds of

African American history programs, celebrations and religious studies.

History scholars and history buffs will readily note that the historical time frame of reference for many of the questions are selectively taken from the 17th-20th centuries, with some exceptions before and after.

For the reader who wants more comprehensive detailed information than provided in the quiz book answers, we have provided a substantial list of primary and secondary references as additional information resources.

The "Ebony Owl, Did You Know" sidebar comments that follow the answers to some of the quiz topics is an attempt on the part of the authors to summarize some of the information in a conclusive and thought provoking manner.

A glossary is also included to help some younger readers and others to better understand the specific meaning and use of certain words and phrases used in the book.

In order to heighten the reader's imaginative reality to the book's content, a number of artistic illustrations of persons and events have been specially drawn and included.

ACKNOWLEDGEMENTS

First, we want to thank the many students who at various grade levels suggested that we write this kind of African American history quiz book.

From opposite ends of the country, from California to Florida, their input and responses through our years of teaching convinced us to write a book that takes a unique approach to inform the reader about African American history and culture.

As professional educators for several decades, we've had the opportunity and the responsibility for organizing, teaching and coordinating various aspects of a multicultural curriculum dealing with Ethnic Studies and African American Studies for various grade levels. One of us has also had the experience of studying and teaching abroad, and both authors have lived in Southeast Asia for nearly five years.

We've also taught related subject matter to various professional groups such as teachers, medical staff, correctional and law-enforcement groups, and U.S. Air Force personnel.

As a result of these experiences, we have found that by using the question-answer quiz method of instruction students at all levels seem to be more highly motivated to learn and retain the information presented, rather than when we used more traditional teaching methods.

We are very much indebted to the many authors and scholars whose primary and secondary reference sources were gleaned, cited and used to write the quiz book.

We especially appreciate the encouragement, critiques, and suggestions given to us from Dona Irvin, Lewis Jennings, Maria, Teresa and Robert Leverett, Linda Jolivett, Fatameh Sangabi and Jacquelyn Miller.

Likewise, we are also grateful to the following members of our Combs family, far and near, who made valuable contributions regarding the book: Namely, John, Angela, Kristina, Rudy, Milton Jr., Roy, Tina, and especially granddaughters Simone, Mignon, Nikki, and grandsons David and Anthony, and especially to Edna Combs, loving matriarch of the family, who devoted many hours to carefully editing and proofreading the Quiz Book during the initial stages.

Finally, we thank Mark Weiman and Roslyn Abraham of Regent Press for their expert help regarding some aspects of the design work and mechanics related to publishing the Quiz Book. It has been a very gratifying experience to work with them on this publication.

SIGNIFICANT AFRICAN AMERICAN HISTORY & CULTURE QUIZ TOPICS

PART ONE:

QUIZ QUESTIONS

QUIZ 1

African American Ancestral, Cultural and Geographical Roots

1. According to modern scientists, what two locations in Africa are the ancestral birthplaces for all human beings?

2. Approximately how many major ethnic (tribal) groups exist in present-day Africa, and in what ways are they different?

3. From about 300 to 1450 C.E., what were the three great African kingdoms in West Africa that existed in sub-Saharan Africa (the Sudan), and who were their leaders?

4. What systems of law and order existed in West African countries prior to European colonization of the region?

5. Describe some examples of West African artistic and cultural expressions when Europeans first made contact with them?

6. What world-renowned European artist acknowledged his use of an African art form in some of his famous drawings?

7. Name some examples of the farming and other occupational skills of Africans who were taken into slavery by Europeans beginning in the 16th century?

8. What was the religious background of African slaves taken to New World colonies?

9. From what regions in Africa were most Africans taken into slavery and then transported to European New World colonies?

10. How large is the continent of Africa in square miles compared to the U.S., to Europe, and to Asia? Also, what is the total population of Africa compared to the U.S., Europe and Asia? And currently, what is the population of Africa compared to the U.S., Europe, and Asia?

1. What is the name of the great Mongol military leader of part African ancestry who, according to ancient Chinese history, led his armies to successfully conquer many parts of the Roman Empire, Asia and China in the 5th century?

2. As a young man he left his country, Haiti, and went to France in 1827, where he wrote two of the world's greatest adventure novels, "The Three Musketeers" and the "Count of Monte Cristo." What is the name of this famous author?

3. The Bible describes her as "black and comely," and as one of the great loves of King Solomon, for whom she bore a son. She held a position of royalty in her own country. What is this woman's name, and where is she mentioned in the Bible and the Qur'an?

4. Name this beautiful and brilliant Egyptian queen who had intimate romantic relationships with two of Rome's great rulers, Julius Caesar, and his successor, Mark Antony. She had children by both men. What names did they give their children?

5. Name the 4th century high-ranking Roman military leader of African ancestry who was in charge of the Roman Emperor's Theban Legion, and who because of his refusal to wage war against Christians living in what is now eastern Germany was executed, and then later ironically declared a saint in the Roman Catholic Church.

6. In the 1700s, two African children, a sister and brother, were kidnapped from their West African village and sold into slavery. Later, the brother bought his freedom, became fluent in English, and wrote one of the first autobiographical and insightful accounts about the tyranny of African slavery. He is often referred to by what two different names?

7. Name two cities in eastern U.S., and one in Canada, that are named for a late 18th century racially-mixed woman from a royal German family who was the wife and Queen of King George III of England. Although she was of noticeably African and German descent, artists usually painted her with a white complexion and European features.

8. Name the legendary African leader who in 1804 led a successful revolution of thousands of African slaves to gain their freedom from France, and develop their own independent country of Haiti.

9. What is the name of the West African prince who led one of the first successful slave and Mexican Indian rebellions against the Spanish in Vera Cruz, Mexico, in the early 1600s? Each year, in the town named after him, there are festive celebrations commemorating their ancestors' historic fight for freedom.

10. Name the person who is considered to be the father of Russian poetry and a great novelist in the 18th century. What are titles of two of his best-known writings? His father was Abram Hannibal, a former African boy slave, who won favor and freedom from Tsar Peter the Great, and eventually became a prominent Russian military leader.

QUIZ 3
African and African American Diaspora and Migration

1. What recent scientific research evidence indicates that many thousands of years ago Africans migrated into China and are the direct ancestors of some Chinese?

2. What large ethnic group populations in South India and Sri Lanka are considered by some scientists to have African ancestors?

3. Name the racially mixed African military leader (247-183 B.C.E.) from Carthage, North Africa, who is considered to be one of the greatest tactical military leaders of his time. He led thousands of his army and dozens of elephants through the Alps mountains in Europe and successfully waged war against the Romans.

4. What archaeological evidence exists that some African-like people may have sailed and settled in Central America long before European explorations to the New World, and established a civilization in that area between 800-400 B.C.E.?

5. What two European countries were the first to forcibly transport large numbers of Africans to its New World colonies to work as slaves in the 1500s?

6. In the 1600s, where, and for what reasons were Africans first brought to the English colonies?

7. What is meant by the term "seasoning" of slaves as it relates to the African slave trade?

8. After the American Revolutionary War, why did some African slaves and free persons emigrate from mainland English colonies and settle in Nova Scotia, Canada?

9. When, where, and for what reasons, did the first group of African Americans emigrate from the U.S. and settle in Africa?

10. In the 19th and 20th centuries why did thousands of African Americans migrate from the southeastern part of the U.S., and settle in what other regions of the country?

QUIZ 4

African People's Active Participation in Spanish, French, Dutch and English Colonies in North America

1. During the 1500s, who was the Spaniard of African ancestry who traveled into the southwestern region of the U.S. (now Arizona and New Mexico), became an interpreter of some of the Native American tribal languages, and as a result helped the Spanish to colonize the area?

2. Name the African slave and body servant (valet) of William Clark, who was an important member of the Lewis and Clark's Northwest Expedition in the early 1800's. What happened to him after the expedition?

3. What is the name of the man of French African background who settled near Lake Michigan in 1765 in a place called "Eschikagou" by the Indians? He was a fur trapper, had a trading post business, and is now considered to be the founder of Chicago.

4. What type of work did African slaves do in the Dutch colony of "New Netherlands," and how did it compare to the kind of work that slaves did in the English colonies of North America?

5. What evidence is there that the first generation of African settlers in the Virginia colony did not come directly from Africa?

6. Name the person who is now considered to be the first African American born in the colony of Virginia in the 1600s.

7. Who is considered to be one of the first African American settlers among the Pilgrims in Plymouth, Massachusetts, in the 1600s?

8. At the time of the American Revolution, what were ten different occupations slaves were usually working at in the English colonies, in addition to those working on plantations?

9. In 1750, which two English colonies in North America had the largest number of slaves, which one had the least, and why?

10. During the first half of the 19th century which of the following European countries, England, France, Portugal, or Spain, had the most and least number of African slaves in its New World territories?

QUIZ 5

African American Slaves and "Quasi-Free" Citizens in the English Colonies and the United States Before the Civil War

1. According to the first census taken in the U.S. in 1790, what was the total slave population, and what percent of the total U.S. population was this?

2. Without using the words "slave" or "slavery" in the new U.S. Constitution of 1787, what were three indirect references that were made regarding slavery?

3. Until the U.S. Constitution was amended in the 1860s, how were the vast majority of people of African ancestry legally defined?

4. What is meant by the term "quasi-free" when applied to those African Americans who were not slaves, and what kind of rights did they generally have compared to others?

5. What does "manumission" mean, and what were three different ways that a slave could become "manumitted"?

6. In South Carolina how much money would the average productive adult slave have to pay for his or her freedom?

7. What were the first 5 states in the U.S. to abolish slavery within their jurisdictions and for what reasons?

8. Who was Dred Scott, and in 1857 what decision did the U.S. Supreme Court make regarding his citizenship status under the U.S. Constitution, and afterwards what were some of its unfavorable consequences for many African Americans?

9. What were the three major export crops planted, cultivated and harvested by plantation slaves in the South prior to the Civil War, and which crop brought the most profit to their owners and why?

10. According to the best estimates of scholars writing about the economics of slavery in the U.S. for the year 1850, how many millions of dollars in lost wages and monetary benefits did all African American slaves lose, or suffer as a net economic loss in that year alone?

QUIZ 6

Freedom Fighters, Patriots and Heroes in the American Revolution War of Independence

1. Name and briefly describe the background of the African American who was among the first colonists shot and killed by British soldiers in the "Boston Massacre" of 1770, an event that helped to precipitate the Revolutionary War.

2. Name the two men, one slave and one free, who fought with colonial militias in Massachusetts during the Revolutionary War, and who also became heroes in battles against the British. One fought in the battle at Bunker Hill, the other fought at Lexington.

3. When General George Washington crossed the Delaware River in a boat to launch the Continental Army's successful attack against British and German forces on Christmas Day, 1775, what two African American oarsmen accompanied him?

4. Name Gen. George Washington's trusted slave valet who served him during the Revolutionary war. What became of him after the war?

5. What is the name of this young African American slave whose cunning efforts as a spy for the French and Continental forces helped them defeat the British in the battle at Yorktown, Virginia?

6. What is the name of the one and only all-African American company of soldiers who fought throughout the Revolutionary War, and after the war, were honored by John Hancock and George Washington for their courage and devotion?

7. Name the all-African company of French soldiers from Haiti who fought with the American Revolutionary Army against the British. Who was their young French Army commander?

8. Who are two little known African American heroines of the Revolutionary War? One of them officially served as a soldier in the Continental army, and the other helped to prevent Gen. George Washington from being assassinated in a plot to poison his food.

9. Name the slave who heroically fought in the place of his master in a Georgia Artillery Corps. He fought in a number of battles against the British in the South.

10. Approximately how many African Americans, free and slave, fought for American Independence in the Continental Army and its militia, and how many fought on the opposing side for the British?

QUIZ 7
United States Colonization in Africa

1. In the early 1800s, what group of Americans emigrated from the U.S. and established the first and only American colony ever in Africa?

2. Why did Americans establish this colony in Africa, and what non-governmental organizations played a significant role in supporting this effort?

3. In the early 1800s, what did the U.S. Congress do to help support the first and only American colony in Africa and its eventual establishment as a nation?

4. In 1847, what official name was given to this colony and nation, and after what American was its capitol city named?

5. Today, what is the size of Liberia in square miles, and what state in the U.S. is comparable in size?

6. Today, what is the estimated total population of Liberia, what is its official language, and what are three of its largest ethnic tribal groups?

7. Since its establishment, what form of government does Liberia have, and what is distinctive about its creation compared to many other countries in Africa?

8. What are the three largest religious groups in Liberia?

9. Who was elected to six consecutive terms as president of Liberia?

10. In 1997, what happened to the elected president of Liberia, and what is the status of its government today?

QUIZ 8

Runaway Slaves and the Underground Freedom Train

1. What is the origin and meaning of the term, "Underground Railroad" (U.G.R.R.), and what are some examples of code words that were used to refer to some of its operations?

2. Approximately when did the "Underground Railroad" begin its operations, and what religious denomination took the lead in supporting it?

3. Name three states in the U.S. that had frequently-traveled escape routes for slaves traveling on the U.G.R.R..

4. What are some examples of the methods and techniques that were used to help slaves escape?

5. What are two of the most spectacular and daring slave escapes that are often cited?

6. Name the courageous and cunning Maryland slave who successfully led more than 300 slaves to freedom on the U.G.R.R.. Although lacking a formal education, this person also became a very influential and highly respected leader on behalf of African Americans.

7. What is the name of the influential African American "Stationmaster" in Philadelphia who helped hundreds of runaways to escape, and was responsible for organizing a great deal of support for the U.G.R.R.? In 1872 he published "Underground Railroad," the first book of its kind describing the activities of the U.G.R.R movement.

8. Name the titles of three songs that were sung by slaves and others as "code songs" as a means of informing each other about the activities and operations of the U.G.R.R..

9. About how many slaves are estimated to have successfully escaped from the slave South by traveling on the U.G.R.R. between 1810-50, and what would be the approximate monetary value of all of them during this period?

10. What political and other actions did southern slave owners and politicians take in order to prevent slaves from running away, and to also insure that they were returned to their owners once apprehended?

QUIZ 9

Institutional Slavery, Racial Segregation and Discrimination in the U. S. Before, During and After the Civil War

1. Answer the following related questions:
    a. What is meant by "institutional slavery?"
    b. What were some of the main reasons for the development of institutional slavery in the U.S. between 1660-1865?
    c. What are some of the damaging, divisive and unresolved consequences of institutional slavery for African Americans and American society?

2. When the Civil War began in 1861, what states had laws prohibiting the practice of slavery, and which ones permitted it?

3. Which of the following actions put an effective end to institutional slavery throughout the U.S., and why?
    a. President Abraham Lincoln's "Emancipation Proclamation."
    b. The 13th Amendment to the U.S. Constitution.

4. What impact did the 14th and 15th Amendments to the U.S. Constitution have on the lives and status of African Americans following the Civil War?

5. When Congress passed the Civil Rights Acts in 1866, what were at least five specific citizenship rights that were enacted for the benefit of African Americans?

6. What were the "Black Codes" in the South, and what impact did they have on the rights and freedoms of African Americans for many decades until Congress passed the Civil Rights Act of 1964?

7. Until the mid-20th century what was the position of the major U.S. labor unions toward representing African American workers?

8. What landmark U.S. Supreme Court decision effectively made institutional racial segregation and discrimination unconstitutional in the U.S.?

9. What former U.S. President and his wife threatened to withdraw membership from their home church because of its decades-old practice of discriminating against African Americans and not allowing them to join the church?

10. When did the active recruitment and integration of African American athletes begin to take place in the professional sports of baseball, basketball and football, and for what reasons?

QUIZ 10

Dedicated and Militant Anti-Slavery Leaders and Organizations in the 18th and 19th Centuries

1. Where was the first anti-slavery organization established in the U.S., and who were some of its prominent leaders? When?

2. Name the founding father who is considered by historians to be one of America's greatest inventors, scientists, statesman and a staunch abolitionist in the 18th century.

3. What is the name of the former African American slave who was self-taught, and who became a very outspoken abolition leader, newspaper publisher and influential African American leader before and during the Civil War? Also, what is the name of the widely read anti-slavery newspaper he and another prominent African American began to publish?

4. In 1830, who published a widely read and circulated pamphlet in the South that urged slaves and others to take militant action against slave owners and the slave system?

5. Give the name and background of an African American clergyman who as a keynote speaker at the first National Negro Convention in 1843 in Buffalo, New York, shocked the audience when he urged them to resist slavery by "any means necessary," even by revolting.

6. Born in the late 1700s in upstate New York, this former slave was one of the most traveled and effective anti-slavery speakers in the abolition movement.

   As a former slave she and her children had been brutalized, and greatly suffered under the slave system. Yet, despite these experiences, she herself maintained an indomitable spirit in the quest for freedom.

   Name this woman who showed such great courage and fortitude.

7. Name two men who carefully planned large-scale slave revolts, one in the vicinity of Charleston, South Carolina, and the other at Richmond, Virginia, only to have them revealed to the authorities by informant slaves before the revolts could be carried out.

8. Name the slave who led a well-organized violent rebellion of slaves that resulted in more than fifty white slaveholding family members being killed in Southampton, Virginia in 1831.

9. In the fall of 1859, who was the highly religious and militant outspoken antislavery leader who led an organized interracial group of men to attack the federal arsenal at Harper's Ferry, Virginia, and what was the outcome of their efforts?

   Also, what very moving American folk song was written to honor him after his death, and often sung by Union soldiers, and is still sung by many today?

10. Name two colleges in the Midwest where white students were some of the first active supporters of the anti-slavery movement in the 1830s.

QUIZ 11

African Americans Who Fought, and Others Who Were Unlikely Heroes and Heroines During the Civil War

1. Name two prominent African American leaders who had a great deal of influence on President Abraham Lincoln in persuading him to recruit free African Americans and emancipated slaves to serve in the Union Armed Forces during the Civil War.

   Also, when did Lincoln finally give official permission to allow African American men to become soldiers in the Union Army?

2. What official name was given to the branch of the Union Army (UA) that organized African American soldiers into five racially segregated artillery, cavalry, infantry and engineering regiments? Also, how many served in the Union Navy, and in other wartime services?

3. What is the name of the USCT regiment that received official recognition for its exceptional bravery in a crucial battle with Confederate forces at Fort Wagner, South Carolina, and who was their young commander?

4. Name the African American slave who became a naval hero after he almost single-handedly and cleverly captured a Confederate war vessel, and then turned it over to the Union side. Also, what were some of his important achievements after the war?

5. Identify two crucial battles that the USCT fought in during the last year of the Civil War, which resulted in the defeat of Confederate forces and helped to end the war.

6. How many Congressional Medals of Honor were given to USCT servicemen for their valor during the Civil War, and who were the first two to receive the award?

7. What was the total number of African American men who were commissioned officers in the Union Army?

8. Identify three little-known women, one of whom was a spy, one of whom was very loyal and influential to the Lincolns, and a third whose volunteer actions greatly helped the Union during the war.

9. In addition to her legendary exploits to assist runaway slaves, what were some of the other specific courageous and dangerous activities that Harriet Tubman took part in to assist the Union Army and to help the war effort?

10. Today, more than a century after the Civil War, where is the national monument located that is specifically dedicated as a memorial to those African Americans who served in all wars, including the Civil War, and up through the Vietnam War?

QUIZ 12

The Gallant Service of the "Buffalo Soldiers" in the U.S. and Abroad

1. Following the Civil War, thousands of U.S. Colored Troop Soldiers were organized into what four regiments. Why did they become known as "Buffalo Soldiers?"

2. What were the main responsibilities and military tasks for the Buffalo Soldiers, especially for the 9th and 10th Cavalries?

3. Generally, what was the background of most of the men who were Buffalo Soldiers?

4. Who were the first commanding officers of the 9th and 10th Cavalries, and what were their attitudes toward the Buffalo Soldiers?

5. Name two major Indian-U.S. wars the Buffalo Soldiers fought and won.

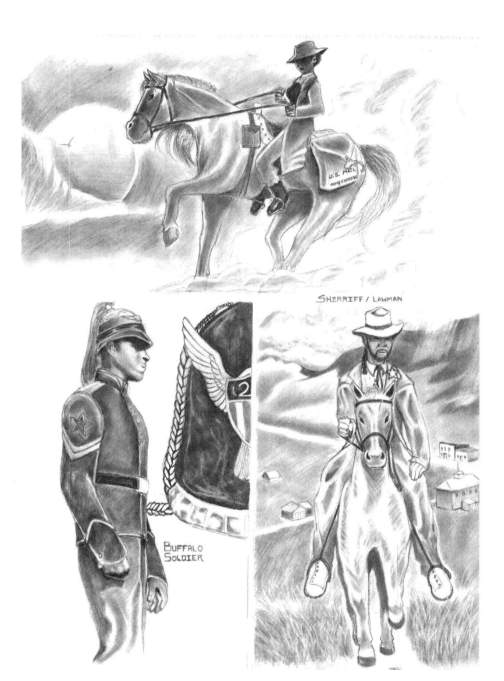

SHERRIFF / LAWMAN

BUFFALO
SOLDIER

6. In what specific ways did the Buffalo Soldiers help facilitate settlement of the western U.S. after the Civil War?

7. What kind of reputation did the Buffalo Soldiers have among the settlers and the various American Indian tribes, and what were some of the official honors they received?

8. What future U.S. President fought with Buffalo Soldiers from the 9th Cavalry in San Juan, Cuba during the Spanish-American War of 1898, and what views did he express toward them? Also, in what other places outside of the U.S. have the Buffalo Soldiers served?

9. "Black Jack" was a nickname given to what U.S. Army general because of his many years as commander of Buffalo Soldiers and other African American troops?

10. When and where was a national monument dedicated to honor Buffalo Soldiers, and who were the keynote speaker and some of the dignitaries in attendance?

1. One of the most colorful and picturesque men of the western frontier of the late 1800s was "Deadwood Dick." What was his real birth name, where was he born, and what were some highlights of his life as a cowboy?

2. Name the Oklahoma cowboy who is credited with introducing "bulldogging" in rodeo shows. What are some highlights of his career and achievements as a rodeo performer?

3. Name the Oregon cowpuncher who was the first African American to win a national "horse bucking" contest in the early decades of the 20th century. What recognition was he given in 1969?

4. When and where were Cherokee Bill and Ben Hodges considered outlaws, and what were their reputations?

5. In the mid-1870s, who was the African American lawman who became one of the most respected U.S. marshals in the West, and especially in the lawless town of Yankee Hill, Colorado?

6. Name two African American men who are considered to be the first, and two of the best, Pony Express riders in California in the 1800s.

7. Name the robust middle-aged African American woman who was the first woman in Montana to carry U.S mail, and to be a stagecoach and freight carriage driver. Also, briefly describe some of her noted characteristics.

8. In 1821, an African American mountaineer discovered a safer and less dangerous pass through the Sierra Nevada Mountains than the Donner Pass. What is his name, and what are some other interesting things about his background?

9. What is the name and background of this free African American who fled from the new slave state of Missouri, and then led one of the first integrated groups of westward settlers to reach the Oregon Territory in 1845? Clue: Except for his middle name, he has the first and last name of a late 20th century U.S. president.

10. During the latter half of the 1800s, about how many African American cowboys are estimated to have ridden as cowpunchers, range hands, cattle rustlers, etc. in the western U.S.? And today, how many are registered with the National Black Cowboys Association (NBCA)?

QUIZ 14

The Origin of Early African American Churches and Pioneer Religious Leaders

1. What are some of the main reasons for the origin and development of separate African American churches in the U.S., and currently, what five African American church denominations have the largest memberships?

2. When and where was the first African American Methodist Episcopal Church organized in the U.S., and who was elected its bishop?

3. Who are considered to be pioneer religious leaders and organizers of the first Baptist churches among African Americans in the U.S?

4. Who is credited with organizing the first African American Zion Church in the U.S., when and where?

5. What is the name of the former Revolutionary War militiaman who became the first ordained and theologically educated African American minister and preacher in the all-white Congregational Church in the U.S. in the late 1700s?

6. Name two prominent religious leaders who are considered pioneers in carrying out Christian missionary work in Africa during the early 1800s. One represented the Richmond African Baptist Missionary Society, and the other the African Methodist Episcopal Church.

7. When, and who, was the first African American priest to be appointed a bishop in the Roman Catholic Church in the U.S.? Also, what is the name of his brother, who became the first African American president of what university in Washington D.C. at the same time?

8. What is the name of the first order of African American Catholic nuns, and when and where were they organized?

9. Name two men who were appointed by President Abraham Lincoln to serve as Chaplains for the United States Colored Troops (USCT) during the Civil War. What were some of their own individual notable achievements after the war?

10. Who were the first African American man and woman to be appointed bishops in the Episcopal Church in the U.S.? When?

QUIZ 15

Little Known Ingenious African American Inventors, Engineers, Medical Doctors and Scientists

1. Born in New Orleans of mixed African and French background, he went to France where he received an engineering education. This enabled him to invent and patent a machine that radically improved the sugar refining process. It was revolutionary and brought great profits to the U.S. and the worldwide sugar industry in the 19th century. What is his name?

2. This man's engineering ability resulted in more than thirty of his inventions being used to upgrade the electrical, mechanical, safety, and communications systems of the railroad industry in the late 1800s. He was born in Columbus, Ohio, and was self-educated. What is his name?

3. In 1881, he helped invent a wire filament for Thomas Edison's incandescent light bulb that made it longer lasting and a brighter source of light. During his long career he became a highly recognized inventor, electronics engineer and consultant. He patented many inventions that he sold to American Bell Telephone, General Electric and Westinghouse companies. He also took an active part in civil rights issues for African Americans and immigrants. What is his name?

4. He invented the prototype for the automatic traffic light system used worldwide today, and also invented an early type of gas mask that was used to rescue nearly thirty workers in a 1916 Erie Canal tunnel accident. What is the name of this ingenious man who had very little formal engineering education, and whose father was an emancipated slave?

5. In the late 1800s this doctor is considered to be one of the first surgeons in the U.S. to successfully perform open-heart surgery. He is also given credit for greatly improving medical services at the Freedmen's Hospital in Washington D.C., and Providence Hospital in Chicago. What is his name?

The African American Quiz Book

6. Name the medical doctor and scientist who developed a new and efficient method to process blood plasma, an innovation that helped to save the lives of many Allied soldiers and others during World War II.

    Tragically, while in the prime of life at age 46, he died shortly after an auto accident in North Carolina.

    There are some conflicting views about whether he did or did not receive proper immediate emergency care at a white hospital where he was first taken after the accident. Even though he was transported to an African American medical facility, there are those who believe that the delay may have resulted in his death.

7. Name the famous Tuskegee Institute botanist and agricultural scientist whose research resulted in the development of a variety of food products that could be derived from peanuts, pecans and sweet potatoes.

    The scope of his scientific work greatly benefited the growth of agriculture in the South and in other parts of the world, and because of this he eventually received worldwide recognition.

    Today, millions of children and adults in the U.S. and around the world enjoy eating one of the food products he discovered. Name it.

8. Before most people had electric refrigerators and freezers in their homes, this man patented the icebox refrigerator in 1891 that kept the temperature inside a specially built box cold when ice was put into it.

   What is this inventor's name? And years later, what other African American invented the first electric refrigerator?

9. It is a common sight to see a street-sweeping vehicle cleaning the parking spaces of a shopping mall and a freeway. What is the name of the African American man who invented a prototype of the modern street sweeper in 1890?

10. Tiger Woods, Jack Nicholas, Nancy Lopez, and Lee Trevino are just some of the great U.S. champion golfers, all of whom use the golf tee. But very few people know that it was an African American Harvard University college graduate who invented the golf tee in 1899. What is his name?

QUIZ 16

Trailblazers and Visionary Leaders
in American Education

1. This man graduated from Middlebury College in Vermont in 1827 and is considered to be the first African American college graduate. Later he became a clergyman in the Congregational Church and also a pioneer educator in Vermont. What is his name?

2. After graduating from Ohio's Oberlin College in 1856, she took a teaching position at Wilberforce College. She is considered to be the first African American college graduate and college teacher in the U.S.. Who is she and what are some interesting facts about her background?

3. This man is now recognized as one of America's greatest educators in 19th century. What is his name, his family background, when and where did he complete his education?

   He wrote an autobiographical book entitled, "Up From Slavery," and established the groundwork for what outstanding university in Alabama?

---

4. After the Civil War, what educational institution was established for African Americans in Washington D.C., and who was appointed its first president?

   Nearly sixty years later as a university, who became its first African American president, and how did his leadership help the school?

5. Today she is recognized as one of America's great educators and humanitarians in the early 20th century. She was director of minority affairs in President F.D. Roosevelt's administration, and was a representative to the United Nations in 1945. She also became president of a number of national African American women's organizations, and founded a college in Florida. Who was this great American?

6. Name the outstanding scholar, educator, and social scientist who was the first African American to graduate with a Ph.D. from Harvard University in 1896.

In 1903 he published, "The Souls of Black Folk," which is still widely read and considered relevant today.

In 1910 he became one of the first non-white executive officers of the newly created NAACP, and editor of the organization's official publication — the "Crisis" magazine, which is still published and widely circulated today.

He is now considered to be one of America's and the world's greatest intellectuals because of his life-long dedication to social science research and writing, and in some ways a pioneer in the field of sociology.

7. What is the name of the person who founded what outstanding independent preparatory boarding schools for African American children in Mississippi in 1909?

Today, this pioneer school has progressed into a 2,000-acre campus with modern buildings and teaching facilities. It has an excellent faculty, is fully accredited, offers a grades 9-12 academic and vocational training curriculum, and receives support from a cross-section of Americans.

On average it educates some 300 students coming from various parts of the U.S. and other countries, and each year a number of top-rated colleges and universities recruit its graduates.

8. Name the former outstanding educator and president of Morehouse University in Atlanta, Georgia, who was a very influential role model and mentor for his student, Martin L. King, Jr., as well as an advisor to a number of civil rights leaders and government officials.

He was also author of two pioneering scholarly books about African American religion: the "Negro's Church" and the "Negro's God."

9. Name two notable African American women trailblazers in education who were selected superintendents of two large urban school districts in the U.S., and briefly describe their background and achievements.

10. Name the African American educator who was one of the first to organize pioneering programs in special education, especially for educationally handicapped children. Both of her parents were teachers in North Carolina. She had a graduate degree from Georgia's Atlanta University, and completed graduate studies at Columbia University. One of her important life achievements was being elected president of the National Education Association (NEA) in the 1960s.

1. What is meant by the term, "Historical Black Colleges and Universities" (HBCU), and during what time period, and for what reasons were most of them founded?

2. Currently, how many HBCUs are there in the U.S., and how many students are enrolled and graduated in these schools each year?

3. In what region of the U.S., and in what states are most HBCUs located, and why?

4. What is the name of the oldest HBCU in the U.S., who founded it, and who have been three of its outstanding graduates? One as a Supreme Court justice; one as a leader in Africa, and one as a bishop in the United Methodist Church.

5. Since its founding in 1867, this HBCU has expanded its excellent academic programs at the undergraduate, graduate, and professional doctoral degree programs, and is rated among the best educational institutions in the nation.

    In the beginning this present HBCU received much of its funding from the federal government channeled through the Freedman's Bureau and educational support from religious groups.

    However, today this HBCU receives most of its financial funding from various kinds of private and public grants, non-profit foundations, student tuitions, and alumni and friends.

    What is the name of this highly rated HBCU whose graduates have provided outstanding leadership in the U.S. and abroad?

6. In 1868, what HBCU was founded in Virginia as a training institute by a Union Army officer for the education of former slaves and American Indians?

    Also, what is the name of one of its most outstanding graduates who established a similar school in Alabama in the 1880s?

7. Name five renowned graduates of the same nationally recognized HBCU who have made outstanding achievements as follows:
   a. World famous civil rights leader
   b. Mayor of Atlanta, Georgia
   c. Georgia state legislator
   d. Movie and television star
   e. Award winning film maker

8. The famous U.S. Army Air Force 99th Fighter Pursuit Squadron had its training base at what HBCU during WWII. As a result what nickname was given to the squadron?

   Also, name two of its graduates who were awarded the Distinguished Flying Cross and were the first African Americans to achieve the rank of general in the U. S. Air Force.

9. In what states are the following ten HBCUs located, when were they founded, and currently what is the approximate size of their enrollments?

   a. AAMU
   b. Bethune-Cookman College
   c. Dillard University
   d. FAMU
   e. Jackson State University
   f. Johnson C. Smith University
   g. Shaw University
   h. Spelman College
   i. Wilberforce University
   j. Xavier University

10. Name at least five significant contributions HBCUs have made to American society.

*Sources of Notable Charitable Giving
for African American
Higher Education: Past and Present*

1. In the 1800s, what two multi-million dollar American industrialists and philanthropists donated thousands of dollars to fund Tuskegee Institute?

2. Name the Jewish American millionaire mail-order businessman who designated part of his charitable funds to improve education for African Americans, as well as promote better race relations for all Americans.

3. Name the U.S. Christian religious denominations that founded and largely funded the following HBCUs:
    a. Howard University in Washington, D.C.
    b. Johnson C. Smith University in Charlotte, North Carolina.
    c. Lincoln University in Pennsylvania.
    d. Morehouse College in Atlanta, Georgia.
    e. Xavier University in New Orleans, Louisiana.

4. In 1944, what African American educator had the vision to create a non-profit charitable organization for the sole purpose of soliciting donations to help support HBCUs?

   Each year millions of dollars are raised by this organization to help provide scholarships for thousands of college students attending HBCUs.

5. Name the national women's sorority of educators founded in 1913 in Washington, D.C., that raises and contributes millions of dollars each year to support various education programs at HBCUs through scholarships, community service and civic activities.

6. Who was the U.S. oil billionaire who donated 5 million dollars to UNCF in 1950?

7. Name at least five multi-million dollar foundations that make regular large contributions to UNCF.

8. What is the name of the African American celebrity entertainer and his wife who since 1988 have regularly contributed millions of dollars to HBCUs and other institutions of higher learning?

9. What is the name of the well-known singer and entertainer who regularly hosted the annual UNCF fundraisers for 25 years?

10. Identify at least ten major African American foundations that contribute thousands of dollars each year for student scholarships and other African American causes that are known to many Americans.

*Extraordinary African American Business
Men and Women Who
Beat the Odds and Shared
Their Wealth With Others: Then and Now*

1. In the late 1700s, this son of a Native American woman and a former slave built a very profitable diversified fishing and shipping business on the coast of Massachusetts. He gave part of his wealth to build a school for free African American children in New Bedford, Massachusetts, because they were not allowed to attend the white schools.

    Disheartened by the racial politics and practices in the newly created U.S., he decided to give both financial support and the use of his ships to transport a "Back to Africa" migration movement to Sierra Leone, West Africa. Who was this man of conscience and good will?

2. At the age of fifteen, this Pennsylvania teenager was handling gun power for cannons on an American Navy vessel.

   After his capture by the British and serving time in prison, he returned to Philadelphia and eventually became the owner of profitable sail-making business. He used part of his earnings to support the American Anti-Slavery Society, to encourage civil rights activities, and to improve education for children in the early 1800s. He was against the "Back to Africa" movement. Name this Philadelphian businessman.

3. Born two years after the Civil War in Richmond, Virginia, she worked very hard as a teenager to support herself, complete her education, and become a teacher. She developed an excellent reputation working as executive secretary for the Independent Order of St. Luke Society that functioned like a mutual aid society to take care of the sick and dying.

   Eventually, she and others established the St. Luke Bank and Trust Company, one of the first African American banks in Richmond.

   Today it is the Consolidated Bank and Trust Company in Richmond. Who was this pioneer and innovative woman banker?

4. In the early 1900s, this woman was one of the first African American millionaires in the U.S.

She became rich when she invented and developed some hair products to beautify women's hair, especially that of African American women.

From the very beginning, she worked extremely hard, walking door-to-door selling her hair pomade products, including an innovative hair straightening hot comb.

She was so successful that her hair products businesses were started in cities like Denver, Indianapolis, Pittsburgh and New York's Harlem, and she became quite wealthy.

Although considered by some to be a conspicuous spender because of the large house and luxurious car she bought, and her elegant lifestyle, she was in fact a very prudent manager of her business affairs, and a generous philanthropist. She donated thousands of dollars for youth scholarships, money to help the aged and poor, and financial support to the NAACP. Name this ingenious and benevolent businesswoman.

5. This man's father was a wealthy Danish plantation owner in the West Indies, and his mother was of African ancestry.

   After his father's death, he inherited considerable wealth and decided to go to San Francisco where he made several successful investments that made him a millionaire.

   He financed a profitable San Francisco Bay ferry steamboat operation, built the city's first hotel, and donated money to build a school.

   Today, a street in downtown S.F. is named after him, and his remains are buried in San Francisco's Mission Delores. Name this adventurous entrepreneur who died at the early age of 38.

6. In the 1850s she was sometimes referred to as another "Madame C.J. Walker" because of her very successful and profitable cosmetics business in the new state of California.

   She traveled near and far from her home in Sacramento doing business and advocating equal rights for African Americans, women and other oppressed groups. She also contributed money to help the disadvantaged. What is her name?

7. What is the name and brief background of the Oklahoma African American with some Creek Indian ancestry who built and brokered million-dollar oil deals in the U.S. and Africa during the first half of the 1900s?

   In addition, other members of the family were politically active at both the state and national levels in demanding freedom of opportunity and equal rights for African Americans and other minority groups, especially in the state of Oklahoma.

8. Name this man who was born nine years after the end of the Civil War to poor farmer parents, but who by 1952 had built the multi-million dollar North Carolina Mutual Life Insurance Company to serve the insurance needs of African Americans who were largely ignored or underinsured by white insurance companies.

9. Born to a poor Alabama family in 1892, this young man began to observe that African Americans were usually denied respectful and decent burial services by white mortuaries.

   Seeing this lack of service, he decided with the help of others to start a burial service and burial society in Birmingham.

   From the increasing profits he made in the mortuary business, he and others established the Citizens Federal Savings and Loan Bank in the city, and eventually it provided funds for home mortgages, especially for African Americans who couldn't get loans elsewhere. What is the name of this innovative businessman?

10. The 2003 "Fortune" magazine named an African American woman in its publication for the first time, and stated that her estimated wealth in dollars was in the billions. Name this extraordinary and talented woman, and give some highlights of her life and background, career achievements, and her contributions to others.

Madame C.J. Walker

Paul Cuffee

Oprah Winfrey

1. Name the first two African American men to serve in the U.S. Senate. For what state during the Reconstruction Period (1865-1877), and under what circumstances did they serve?

2. How many African American men served in the U.S. House of Representatives during the Reconstruction Period?

3. Who was the first African American to serve as governor of what state during the Reconstruction Period?

4. Today, there is a small town and HBCU in Oklahoma named after a highly educated African American who was elected to the U.S. Congress in 1889. What is his full name, what state did he represent, and what were some of his notable achievements?

5. a. Name the first African American ever to be elected both lieutenant governor and governor of what southern coastal state in the latter part of the 20th century.
    b. Name the first two African Americans to be elected lieutenant governors of what states in the 21st century.

6. When and who were the first two African American women to be elected to the U.S. House of Representatives in the 20th century, and briefly, describe some highlights of their political careers?

7. Name and give a brief background of the only three African Americans to be elected to the U.S. Senate.

8. What are the names and dates of the first African Americans elected to be mayors of the following large cities in the U.S.?
    a. Atlanta
    b. Chicago
    c. Detroit
    d. Gary
    e. Los Angeles
    f. Minneapolis
    g. New York
    h. Philadelphia
    i. Washington, D.C.
    j. San Francisco

9. Name the first African Americans appointed to serve in U.S. Presidential cabinet positions as secretaries of what major executive branches of government in the latter part of the 20th century, and name the Presidents who appointed them.

10. Name the African American Congresswoman from Northern California who had the courage not to vote affirmatively to authorize the House of Representatives to support the U.S. President's proposal to invade Iraq in 2003, and because of her action suffered great criticism and unfair attacks from some news media, some of her colleagues, and many others.

QUIZ 21

The NAACP, National Urban League and Other Civil Rights and Community Organizations: A Brief Overview

1. Who organized the National Association for the Advancement of Colored People (NAACP), when, and for what purpose and objectives?

2. Who organized the National Urban League (NUL) in 1910, and for what reasons?

3. Name three African American men who have been very influental organizers and leaders for the Congress of Racial Equality (CORE), and indicate what the organization's main purpose and objectives are?

4. Who organized the Student Non-Violent Coordinating Committee (SNCC), and for what purpose? When did they do so and where did they do it?

5. Why was the Southern Christian Leadership Conference (SCLC) organized in 1957, and who was elected its president and secretary?

6. Name two college students who are credited with organizing the Black Panther Party in Oakland, California in the 1960s. For what reasons?

7. Who founded the Universal Negro Improvement Association (UNIA), what was his background, and what was the purpose and effectiveness of the UNIA? When was it founded?

8. Who is credited with organizing and providing leadership for the first large and successful national labor union for African American railroad workers? When? He was also an advisor for the civil rights movement during the 1950-1960s, and a leading organizer for the 1963 March on Washington D.C.

9. In the late 1700s, who organized the first African American Masonic fraternity in the U.S, for what purpose, and under what circumstances?

10. Name the first and oldest college fraternity for African American men, and first sorority for African American women. Also, why were they founded, and what are their current memberships and types of service programs?

Also, identify some other African American fraternaties and sororities that have very viable and influential programs.

QUIZ 22

Talented and Exceptional Early Writers, Poets, Journalists and Artists

1. This 18th-century African child was kidnapped and sold to a family in Boston, Massachusetts. By the time she was a young teenager, she had learned English, studied Greek and Latin, and become so skilled at writing poetry at such a mature level that she astonished both American and British literary experts.

   Some of her poetry was published, and one of her poems was written for General George Washington. He was so impressed with her ability that she was invited to visit him at his military headquarters in Cambridge, Massachusetts. Who was this precocious young woman?

2. He was self-educated, and in the early 1800s, wrote and published an anti-slavery pamphlet that was widely circulated and read by both whites and blacks. In many parts of the slave south it was considered seditious and was banned. What is the name of the pamphlet and who wrote it?

3. Two men are credited with publishing the first African American newspaper in the U.S. What are their names and backgrounds?

4. Name the former runaway slave who began publishing the antislavery newspaper, "The North Star" in 1847. He also became one of the most powerful speakers and activists for full citizenship rights for African Americans and women.

   Later in his career he was appointed to a number of positions in the U.S. government.

   Today, because of his outstanding achievements, he and his former home are now commemorated at a National Historical site in Washington, D.C.

5. Name the former shoeshine boy who became a wealthy businessman in San Francisco, and who published the city's first African American newspaper in 1855. His editorials were highly critical of California's discriminatory "Black Laws."

6. As a very mature and talented teenager in the 1880s, she was already writing newspaper articles for African American newspapers in Cincinnati and Cleveland, Ohio.

When she moved to Northern California she wrote and published one of the first history books on "The Negro Trailblazers of California."

She was also one of the first African Americans to write for the Oakland Tribune newspaper, and as an outspoken journalist she successfully challenged some white writers and publishers not to use such negative and stereotype reference terms as "darkie" and "nigger" in their writing.

She also wrote and spoke in support of millionaire John D. Rockefeller, Jr.'s, plan to build the International House (IH) building on the University of California's Berkeley campus that would provide housing for all non-white students. They were consistently denied campus housing by the Greek letter fraternities and sororities. Who was this courageous journalist and trailblazer?

7. In the 1890s, who was the courageous woman who published articles in the "Memphis Free Speech" newspaper that exposed the conspiracy and motives of those who were responsible for lynching a number of African American men in Memphis, Tennessee?

   She was also the first African American woman to work with the first NAACP executive committee, and with some early American women's suffrage movements.

   She was given the equivalent nickname, "Pistol Packin Mama," because she would sometimes carry a gun to protect herself from white bigots and terrorists who often threatened her.

8. Name the first African American woman and man to receive the prestigious Pulitzer Prize, and for what kind of literary and artistic work.

9. Give the birth name, and American Indian tribal name, of this famous African American sculptress whose father was African American and mother Chippewa Indian.

Her medallions and sculptures often focused on outstanding Civil War heroes and abolitionists, as well as other persons and historical themes of the 1860-1970s.

Also, name the creative, little-known African American woman impressionist artist whose eye-catching scenes of life in the Carribean, Africa, and the U.S.A. are being recognized for their genius in recent years.

10. What is the name of this world famous African American painter whose works had great appeal in the 1890s? His use of rich colors and realistic style expressed in such paintings as "The Banjo Lesson" and "Daniel in the Lion's Den" earned him many awards in the U.S. and other countries.

1. What is the name of this unusually talented blind slave child who began giving piano recitals at an early age? His owners arranged musical programs for him to play to amazed audiences in the U.S., South America and Europe in the last half of the 1800s.

    He is considered to be one of the first gifted American children of any age or background to play classical piano music before such audiences.

2. Name the famous college singing group from Nashville, Tennessee, that was very popular in the 1870s because of the traditional "Negro Spirituals" they sang to audiences in many parts of the U.S., and in Europe.

    Their concerts greatly helped to generate increased financial support for their college, and equally important, they helped to create a broader awareness and appreciation for a whole new genre of American music.

3. One of the interesting ironies of U.S. history is that in 1878 a northern-born African American songwriter, with help from a co-writer, wrote and published what is now the official state song of Virginia. What is the title of the song, and who wrote it?

4. In 1893, this self-taught musical genius played a concert at the Chicago's World Fair, and in the 20th century he composed and played a new musical genre called the "blues." Name this famous innovative musician, and what are the titles of two of his most popular blues song?

5. What are the names of the three women vocalists whose singing styles in the first half of the 20th century greatly helped to popularize African American blues and jazz music? One was given the title, "Empress of the Blues;" another, "Mother of the Blues;" and the third, "The First Lady of Song."

6. This world-renowned African American was born in 1898 in Rochester, New York, where his father, a runaway slave, and his mother decided to settle.

By the time he was six his mother died and this left quite a void in his young life. However, by the time he finished high school, he had become an excellent student and won a scholarship to Rutgers University.

He was also an outstanding student and leader at Rutgers, and before graduating was selected as a member of the Phi Beta Kappa fraternity because of his academic excellence. In 1917-18 he was a two-time All-American college football player at Rutgers.

After earning a law degree from Columbia University, he became an outspoken advocate for African American civil rights, as well as a highly respected social activist for worldwide human rights. He also became one of America's noted baritone/bass concert singers and actors, appearing in Shakespeare's "Othello." Name this outstanding American.

7. Beginning in the 1930-'40s, what African American woman was considered to have one of the world's greatest contralto and operatic voices?

   When denied an opportunity to sing at Constitution Hall in Washington, D.C., by the Daughters of the American Revolution (DAR) because of its racial policies, her friend, Mrs. Eleanor Roosevelt, made arrangements for her to give a concert at the Lincoln Memorial. She sang before a large crowd of more than seventy thousand. Subsequently, Mrs. Roosevelt withdrew her membership from the DAR.

8. What is the birth name and stage name of this internationally famous jazz pianist-composer and big band orchestra conductor?

   Also, what are the titles of two of his most famous and popular compositions he often played at the Cotton Club in Harlem, New York?

9. She is considered to be one of America's greatest gospel singers because of her soulful singing. In 1963 she sang in Washington, D.C., when Dr. Martin L. King, Jr., gave his famous "I Have a Dream" speech. At Dr. King's funeral in 1968 she sang one of his favorite gospel songs, "Precious Lord Take My Hand." What is her name?

10. Name this world famous trumpet player, vocalist and entertainer whose jazz roots were in New Orleans. His joyful, soulful music has brought happiness to many.

He also was a staunch civil rights advocate who during most of his career refused to entertain for segregated audiences. And when asked to be a "goodwill ambassador" overseas during the 1950s, he refused and said he wouldn't do that until the U.S. government granted full citizenship rights to African Americans.

He also composed and sang a song that became the title of what movie starring Barbara Streisand?

QUIZ 24

Record-Breaking African American Athletes and Sports Champions in the U.S. and the World

1. The annnual Kentucky Derby is one of the most popular sporting events in the U.S., but very few people know that an African American jockey won the Derby three times in the late 1800s. What is his name, and what are some interesting facts about his background?

2. Name the first African American woman to pitch for a professional baseball team. She played with the Indianapolis Clowns in the former Negro Baseball League in the 1940s.

3. As an exceptional four-sport athlete at UCLA, he became the first African American contracted to play professional baseball in the National League in 1947.

   His outstanding career earned him such awards as: "Rookie of the Year," "Most Valuable Player," and election to the Baseball Hall of Fame in 1962. Who is this great American athlete?

   Likewise, name the first African American to play professional baseball in the American League, for what team, and what national award did he receive in the 1990s?

4. Who became the first two African American major league baseball team managers, for what teams and when?

5. a. In 1910, this powerful boxer defeated the highly-rated former U.S. heavyweight-boxing champion, Jim Jeffries, in a fifteen-round bout.

This victory resulted in his becoming the first African American to be recognized as the world heavyweight champion, but it is also set off indiscriminate attacks against African Americans in differnet parts of the country.

The movie "The Great White Hope" was based on his life. What is his name, and what is the name of the actor who portrayed him?

b. In 1938, on the eve of World War II, another great African American heavyweight boxer knocked out Nazi Germany's champion with lightning speed in the first round of their second match. This feat made him an instant American hero. What is his birth name, his boxing nickname, and what is the name of the German boxer he defeated?

c. "Sports Illustrated" magazine selected this charismatic and poetically witty boxing heavyweight champion as the greatest American athlete of the 20th century. What is his name, and what are five of his notable achievements?

6. In 1936, who became the first American, and African American, to win four gold medals in track and field events at the Olympics held in Berlin, Germany?

   Also, 24 years later, who was the first African American woman to win three gold medals in track and field events at the Olympics held in Rome, Italy, in 1960?

7. Who was the first African American tennis player to win the men's singles at Wimbledon in 1975, and the first to be inducted into the Tennis International Hall of Fame?

   Also, long before Serena and Vanessa Williams became world famous tennis champions for the U.S., who was the first African American woman to win the Wimbledon women's singles in 1957?

8. Name the professional basketball player who was the first player in the National Basketball Association (NBA) to score 100 points in a single game. For what team?

   Also, what is the name of his greatest competitor on the basketball court who eventually became the first African American NBA coach in 1966, and for what team?

9. Who were the first African American football players to play as fullbacks for what professional teams in the National Football League, in the late 1940s? When?

   Also, in the late 1950s, who set an all-time record for rushing yards in the NFL after playing nine seasons with his team?

10. Name the first African American athletes to win the 1956 and 1958 Olympic decathlon events. What records did they set?

African Americans Who Are Commemorated On United States Postage Stamps

1. Who was the very first African American to appear on a U.S. postage stamp, and why was this person honored? When?

2. Who was one of the first African Americans to appear on a U.S. postage stamp in the "Black Heritage" series? When?

3. He organized and promoted the first "Negro History Week" in 1926 in the U.S., and nearly sixty years later he was commemorated on U.S. postage stamp. What is his name?

4. In what year did the first nationally and internationally known African American woman appear on a U.S. postage stamp, and what were some of her major accomplishments?

5. In 1995, who was commemorated on a U.S. Black Heritage series postage stamp for being the first African American woman to receive an international pilot's license in 1921? She received it in France.

6. Who was the first African American Nobel Peace Prize winner to be honored on a U.S. postage stamp? As Under-Secretary of the United Nations during the 1950-1960s, he is credited with negotiating one of the first peace treaties between Israel and Palestine.

7. Name the NAACP executive secretary from Minnesota who was honored on a U.S. postage stamp because of his civil rights leadership between 1955-77.

8. What legendary African American cowboy was included in the "Legends of the West" U.S. postage stamp series in 1994?

9. Name three African American jazz and blues singers from the early 20th century who were given recognition on U.S. postage stamps in 1944.

10. What is the name of the only 20th century African American whose image appears on different editions of U.S. postage stamps, and also on more than 100 postage stamps of countries throughout the world?

QUIZ 26

Notable 20th Century African American Armed Services Heroes and Leaders

1. Name the African American sailor who courageously manned an antiaircraft gun on his ship, the USS *Arizona,* and shot down four Japanese enemy planes during the attack on Pearl Harbor, December 7, 1941.

    He was recognized as one of the first heroes of World War II and eventually received the Navy Cross. He was not trained as a gunner but worked in the ship's kitchen.

2. What African American Tank Battalion fought courageously with General Patton's Third Army to help defeat the German Army near the end of WW II?

    It was also one of the first U.S. army units to liberate hundreds of imprisoned Jews at the Nazi holocaust death camps in Dachau and Buchenwald, Germany.

3. This father and son had life-long military careers, and were the first African Americans to achieve the ranks of general in the US. Armed Services.

   The father served in the Spanish-American War, and was promoted through the ranks to Brigadier General.

   His son was a West Point graduate, and went on to distinguish himself as a U.S. Army Air Force pilot and squadron commander in World War II and the Korean War.

   He was also the first African American to command a U.S. Army Air Base, and the first African American to be awarded the Distinguished Flying Cross in 1971. He retired with the rank of Lieutenant General.

   Can you name this father and son career military duo?

4. Name the now-famous first all African American Air Force flying unit that was organized during WW II, and was highly decorated for its hundreds of successful combat missions flown over North Africa and parts of Europe.

5. Born the youngest of seventeen children in Pensacola, Florida, this Tuskegee Airman flew more than 170 combat missions in the Korean and Vietnam Wars, and was awarded Distinguished Flying Cross.

His flying buddies sometimes referred to him as the "Black Panther" of the skies because of his deadly combat flying, his heroism, and ability as one of the Air Force's best pilots.

He became Commander of Travis Air Force Base in Fairfield, California, in the 1970s, where he helped to institute new race relations and nondiscrimination policies for TAFB military personnel in the rental and sale of housing in nearby communities.

He was also made Commander of the North American Defense Command, controlling all air attack forces in the U.S. and Canada.

He went on to become the first African American to achieve a rank of four-star general in the U.S. Army Air Force. He would often cite the following as his eleventh commandment, "thou shall not quit!"

Who was this highly committed and courageous American military hero?

6. How many African American women served in the Women's Army Corps (WACS), and WAVES (Women Accepted for Volunteer Emergency Service) during World Wear II?

7. Name the first and second African American women to receive the rank of general in the U.S. Army.

8. Who was the first African American to command what U.S. Naval warship and achieve the rank of Rear Admiral, and what is his naval training background? When did this happen?

9. Name the first African American to become a four-star Admiral in the U.S. Navy. What was his educational background and training, and what were some of his assignments before achieving this important position?

10. Who was the first African American to achieve the rank of General in the U.S. Marine Corps, and what is his background and military training?

QUIZ 27

Time-Honored Celebrations and Cultural Observances

1. During which month of the year is "Black History" or "African American History" observed by many African Americans and others, and why?

2. Who helped organize the first "Negro History" observances in the U.S. and for what reasons? When?

3. Name an anthem-type song that is often sung during most African American History observances and similar programs. Also, name the composers of the music and lyrics.

4. What is the origin of the "Negro National Flag" or banner, and what is the symbolic meaning of each of its three different colors: red, black and green?

5. What is "Juneteenth," and why is it celebrated by some African Americans and not others?

6. In what year did Congress make Dr. Martin Luther King's birthday an official national holiday in the U.S.?

7. On what date do many African Americans observe Malcolm X's birthday, and for what reasons?

8. What is "Kwanzaa," who created it, and when and why is it observed?

9. Name the seven principles of Kwanzaa and briefly describe the meaning of each.

10. What is "Ramadan," and what groups of African Americans observe it?

QUIZ 28

A Brief Profile of Dr. Martin Luther King, Jr.

1. Where and when was Martin L. King, Jr., born, and what were his mother and father's occupations?

2. Briefly state the historical significance of Martin Luther King's first and middle names.

3. How many grades did Martin L. King "skip" when he was a high school student, and how old was he when he enrolled in college?

4. What was Martin L. King's chosen profession, and when and where did he complete his college and graduate school studies?

5. Who did Martin Luther King, Jr. marry, when and where did they meet, and what are the names of their children?

6. After completing his graduate studies, when and where did the recently ordained Rev. Martin L. King, Jr., go to become pastor of what church?

   Also, what is the name of the minister at this church who took a leading role in the emerging civil rights movement in Montgomery, Alabama, long before King?

7. Although Rosa Parks actually took a very courageous step to defy the law that required racial segregation of bus passengers in Montgomery, and should be honored for doing so, name three other persons who should be equally credited for providing leadership for the Montgomery, Alabama, bus boycott and helping to bring an end to such segregation.

8. As a Christian clergyman and civil rights leader, what kind of philosophy and techniques did Dr. Martin L. King say should be used to bring about social justice and equality for African American people, and for all oppressed people?

9. When, where, and why did Dr Martin L. King, Jr., receive the Nobel Prize for Peace, and what did he do with its monetary reward?

10. After Dr. King made his famous "I Have A Dream" speech, in what southern city was he jailed, and while there, what famous and profound letter did he write to his Christian clergy critics?

1. Give the date and place where Malcolm X was born. What name was he given at birth, and what were his parents like?

2. While growing up in Lansing, Michigan, and in Boston, Massachusetts, what were some traumatic experiences Malcolm had to face during his childhood and youth years?

3. When, and for what reasons, was Malcolm put in jail and prison, and in what ways did these incarceration experiences have an impact on his life?

4. Name two persons who had a great deal of influence on Malcolm becoming a convert to the Muslim religion, and an Imam for the Nation of Islam.

5. During what time period did Malcolm drop his last name, "Little," and use the letter "X" in its place. Why did he do so?

6. When, where, and to whom did Malcolm get married, and what Muslim name did she take? Also, what names did they give their four children?

7. By 1963, what was Malcolm X's leadership and influence in the NOI?

8. At one time, what were Malcolm's views about the nature of white people, their creation, and his reasons for calling them "white devils"?

9. Why did Malcolm X travel to Mecca, Saudi Arabia, in 1964, and what important changes took place in his views about his own Muslim identity, and in some of his views about racial identity?

10. When and where was Malcolm X assassinated, allegedly by whom, and for what reasons?

1. What is the meaning of the following non-english words:
   a. *Allah*
   b. *Islam*
   c. *Muslim*
   d. *Qur'an*
   e. *Mosque*
   f. *Imam*
   g. *Mullah*
   h. *Jihad*
   i. *Ummah*
   j. *As-Salaam 'alaikum* and *Wa-alaikum salaam?*

2. Who is considered the founder of Islamic religion, and when, and where did it begin?

3. Name the Five Pillars of religious faith for all Muslims, worldwide.

4. Currently, it is estimated that how many different African American Muslim religious communities are organized in the U.S.?

5. Who organized the Nation of Islam, when, where and for what reasons?

6. Who is the current leader of the Nation of Islam and what are considered some of his important achievements during the 1990s?

7. Which U.S. city and state is the headquarters of the Nation of Islam, and what is its estimated membership?

8. Who organized the development of the American Society of Muslims in the U.S., and for what reasons? When?

9. Where is the headquarters of the American Society of Muslims located, and what is its estimated membership?

10. Name five nationally prominent African American Muslims who have been successful in any notable career endeavor, in addition to Minister Farrakhan.

QUIZ 31
Debunking Myths and Stereotypes About Race and African Americans

1. Name the 18th-century European scientist who began to classify the human race into what he perceived as the following four absolute racial categories: African, American Indian, Asiatic, and European. Also, what generalizations did he make about his classification of racial groups?

2. Beginning in 1950, how have modern scientists defined race, and why would they reject the use of such words as: black, brown, red, white and yellow to refer to race?

3. Where in the Bible is there any clear reference to distinct racial groups on the basis of skin color?

4. Why do modern geneticists and many other 21st-century scientists reject the idea that racial ancestry determines level of intelligence, other abilities, and achievement in life?

5. Name the chemical substance in all normal human beings, except for a small number, that determines a person's skin, hair and eye color. What is its basic biological function?

6. What is the basis for the "Aryan" or white race superiority theory held in the past by Hitler's German Nazis, and believed today by some groups such as the "Skinheads," "Aryan Brotherhood," and "Ku Klux Klan?"

7. Define and contrast the meanings of "racial mongrelization" and "interracial hybridization."

8. Looking at the history of sports and all athletic activities in the U.S., which of the following groups has generally demonstrated superior athletic ability or athleticism: African Americans, European Americans or Asian Americans, and why?

9. What percent of the U.S. population is estimated to be racially mixed between persons of African and European ancestry? Also, what percent of mixing between African Americans and Native American Indians?

10. Myth or fact? There is sufficient scientific data to indicate that some racial groups are more sexually active than others, If yes, why? If no, why not?

QUIZ 32

Unforgettable Flagrant Acts of Brutality, Dehumanization, Disfranchisement and Terrorism Suffered by African Americans

1. What torturous and extreme methods did some slave traders and slave owners use to identify the slaves in their possession?

2. Ordinarily, what did slave owners do to punish runaway, disobedient or "uppity" slaves?

3. What roles did "overseers" and "drivers" have on slave plantations, and what kind of techniques and methods did they use to get the most out of slave labor?

4. In 1864, what happened to hundreds of African American Union Army soldiers and civilians at Fort Pillow, Tennessee, and who was responsible?

5. Who organized the Ku Klux Klan (KKK) and for what stated purpose and objectives? When and where? Also, what is its current membership?

6. In 1896, what was the case name of the U.S. Supreme Court decision that made "Jim Crow" laws legal, and what landmark Supreme Court decision in 1954 overturned the 1896 Court's decision, and on what basis?

7. What terrible events took place in the following African American communities in the years indicated, and what were the causes and consequences?
   a. Atlanta, Georgia, in 1906.
   b. East St. Louis, Illinois, in 1917.
   c. Tulsa, Oklahoma, in 1921.
   d. Jasper, Texas, in 1998.

8. Who were the following persons and what tragedies happened to them in the state of Mississippi?
   a. Emmett Till (1941-1955).
   b. Medgar Evers (1925-1963).
   c. James Chaney (1943-19640, Andrew Goodman (1944-1964) and Michael Schwerner (1940-1964).

9. On September 15, 1963, about two months before the assassination of President John F. Kennedy, what egregious and dreadful event took place at an African American church in Birmingham, Alabama, and what was the outcome for the victims and the perpetrators?

10. In August 1964, what happened to Lieutenant Colonel Lemuel Penn after he had completed reserve officer's training at Fort Benning, Georgia?

QUIZ 33

Exceptional 20th Century Giants for Equal Rights and Justice in the U.S.

1. Name the father and son clergymen who were staunch civil rights leaders in New York City during the 1940-'50s. The son succeeded his father as pastor of one of the city's oldest and largest Baptist churches. The son was also elected to more than 10 terms in the U.S House of Representatives where he became a very influential advocate for minority civil rights and social justice.

2. Identify this African American man who is now considered to have been one of the most brilliant legal minds and lawyers in the U.S. in the 20th century.

He was born in Washington, D.C., graduated from Amherst College as a Phi Beta Kappa honor student, and then earned his law degree at Harvard University.

His expertise in U.S. Constitutional law and legal strategy greatly helped to undo racial segregation and discrimination in the U.S., especially against African Americans who were segregated and discriminated against in all levels of education and in many parts of public life.

He often advised the NAACP lawyers. As Dean of Howard University's Law School, he enhanced its program and was an important role model and mentor for many of the law school's graduates. Among them was Thurgood Marshall, who later became the first African American U.S. Supreme Court Justice in 1967.

3. As chief lawyer for the NAACP during the early 1960s, she was the first African American woman to win nearly ten civil rights cases brought to the U.S. Supreme Court.

   She was also the first African American woman to be elected to the New York State Senate, and afterwards to be appointed to the U.S. Circuit Court in New York's southern district. Who is she?

4. In 1963, she was the only female member of the Council for United Civil Rights Leadership that planned the famous 1963 March on Washington with keynote speaker, Dr. Martin L. King, Jr.

   After earning degrees from New York University, her career spans many decades as she worked with various civil rights and social justice non-profit organizations. She has served in executive positions with the National Council of Negro Women, the Delta Sigma Theta sorority and the American Red Cross for more than forty years.

   She recently published her memoir, "Open Wide the Freedom Gates," and at age 91 she was elected chair and president emerita of the NCNW. What is the name of this great American woman?

5. Name the visionary woman who took the lead in founding the Children's Defense Fund (CDF) in 1973. It was created for the purpose of identifying and helping to protect the various educational, health and social needs of all children in the U.S.

   She earned her law degree at Yale University and was the fist African American woman lawyer admitted to the Mississippi state bar.

   One of her books, "Families in Peril: An Agenda for Social Change," has become an important guide for government agencies at all levels.

6. She is considered to be one of the most courageous civil rights and political activists in the 1960s.

   At the 1964 Democratic National Convention in Atlantic City, New Jersey, she had the fortitude to challenge the decades-old discriminatory practice of excluding African Americans from Democratic Party politics in Mississippi.

   Her efforts to have the Mississippi Freedom Democratic Party (MFDP) delegates seated was caustically challenged by white Mississippi Dixiecrats, and only two of their seats were officially recognized at the time. But her passionate plea at the convention subsequently helped to change DP politics both in Mississippi and at the national level, leading to a more equitable inclusion of African American delegates in Democratic Party politics as a whole.

7. As a college student he became actively involved with CORE and SCLC in the 1960s, and was a close associate with Dr. Martin L. King, Jr., and today, this high profile African American leader has a worldwide reputation as an influential civil rights activist and humanitarian.

   He helped found such organizations as People United to Save Humanity (PUSH) and the Rainbow Coalition.

   He was also a formidable presidential candidate for the Democratic Party in 1988, and his intervention in a hostage crisis involving Iran during the Reagan administration resulted in the release of some American hostages and prisoners. Who is this dedicated American?

8. In 1957, some three years after the U.S. Supreme Court's landmark school desegregation decision, this courageous woman, in the face of threats and hostility, stood firm to support nine African American students seeking to enroll in the segregated all-white Central High School in Little Rock, Arkansas. President Dwight D. Eisenhower had to send federal troops to Little Rock to protect the students. Who is she?

9. In 1970, she was on J. Edgar Hoover's FBI "most wanted" list as a fugitive from justice, and was arrested and jailed for more than 15 months on charges that she was an accomplice of a failed prison escape and shootout at Solidad State Prison in California.

As the result of a successful legal appeal by attorney Howard Moore, Jr., of Oakland, and working with him as his co-counsel in a much-celebrated trial, she was acquitted and freed.

At the time, there was much speculation that her forthright support of the Black Panther Party, her socialist political philosophy, and her open criticism of the U.S. prison system were the real reasons why various law enforcement agencies were going after her.

Currently, she is a full professor at the University of California, Santa Cruz, and is considered by her peers to be a brilliant scholar. What is her name?

10. Name the Northern California African American legislator whose leadership resulted in the state's first Fair Employment Practices law, passed in 1959, which prohibited racial discrimination in employment, and first "fair housing" law, passed in 1963.

Its implementation, however, was nullified by the passage of the Proposition 14 initiative supported by Gov. Ronald Reagan, only later to be overturned by the California State Supreme Court and the U.S. Supreme Court.

On the other hand, former California Gov. Earl Warren, later Chief Justice of the U.S. Supreme Court, was not only a good friend of this man, but also supported his political efforts to bring about equal opportunity.

Besides serving in the California State Legislature for eighteen years, he was also a pharmacist with his own pharmacy in Berkeley. He earned his degree in pharmacy from UC Berkeley as well as a master of public administration from UCB.

In 1964, one of his highest honors was to receive the outstanding alumnus of the year award from the University of California Pharmaceutical Alumni Association.

QUIZ 34
Courageous White Americans
Who Did the Right Thing

1. In the mid-1700s, a white couple in Boston went to a slave market to buy a slave to do domestic work in their home. After observing a small and frail African girl who had obviously been traumatized by her terrifying kidnapping experience, they felt compelled to buy the seven- or eight-year-old African child.

   Little did they know that in a short time this young child would quickly learn how to read, write and speak English, and that in a few years later she would even be learning Greek and Latin.

   In her teen years she astonished her surrogate parents by her ability to write beautiful and meaningful adult level poetry, some of which was read and recited to General George Washington and audiences in England.

   Name this precious and talented young African poet and her surrogate mother and father who raised her.

2.   In 1833, after raising money on her own, this young private school principal in Canterbury, Connecticut, decided to teach a number of young African American women at her school in spite of the threats and hateful actions coming from some of the people in the local community, even from some local church members.

After more than eighteen months of doing her best to teach her students in what was becoming an extremely hostile and violent environment, she decided to close the school, even though she was continuing to get some support from local Quakers. Who was this courageous young woman who tried to do the right thing?

3. In 1839, more than fifty Africans held captive on the slave ship, *Amistad,* were able to gain control of the ship by killing some of the Spanish crew and forcing them to sail the ship into waters off the North Atlantic coast of Massachusetts.

After being forcibly brought to shore by U.S. naval authorities, some basic questions arose concerning the legal status of these slaves; whether they were still property of the slave ship owners, whether they were free persons who had been wrongly kidnapped from their African villages; and whether the U.S. or Spain had jurisdiction to resolve the matter.

It so happened that a former U.S. President, who was subsequently a member of the U.S. House of Representative, was persuaded and motivated to successfully plead the case on behalf of the Africans before the U.S. Supreme Court.

As a result of his reputation and skill in presenting their plea, the Court granted the slaves their freedom and safe return to Africa.

Earlier in his political career he had been an ardent abolitionist. Who was this man who has been characterized by historians as one of America's most eloquent and venerable statesman?

4. Following the Civil War these two Congressmen were relentless in their demands that the U.S. government provide freed slaves not only full equal rights but also the tangible means to become economically self-sufficient.

   One of the men was a Congressman from Pennsylvania who agreed with the slogan that the emancipated slaves should be given "forty acres and a mule."

   The other man was a Harvard Law school graduate who became a U.S. Senator representing Massachusetts. One of his anti-slavery speeches in the Senate chambers became so provocative that a Senator from South Carolina physically attacked him with a cane on the floor of the Senate. Name these two courageous men.

5. This First Lady and her husband, the 32nd President of the U.S., were the first national leaders in the 20th century to positively and publicly take action to bring about equal opportunity for African Americans.

In 1939, when the all-white Daughters of the American Revolution (DAR) membership organization would not permit a nationally acclaimed African American contralto and opera singer to sing at Constitution Hall, the wife of the President was indignant.

In response to the DAR's action, this First Lady took the initiative, along with others, to have the singer give an open-air concert on the steps of the Lincoln Monument. The concert drew a large audience of 75,000, and subsequently, the First Lady withdrew her membership from the DAR.

At the beginning of summer in 1941, this First Lady's husband, the President of the U.S., issued his Executive Order 8802 that officially prohibited racial discrimination in wartime defense industries.

It was the first time that any U.S. President in the 20th century had taken affirmative action of any kind to provide equal employment opportunity rights for African Americans.

His action was in part influenced by a threatened one-hundred-thousand person "March on Washington" to be led by African American labor leader and activist, A. Philip Randolph.

Who were this very popular and active First Lady, the famous singer, and President of the U.S. during this period?

6. Very few people know that this world famous adventure writer was raised for a period of time by an African American foster mother in West Oakland.

    She saw to it that he went to school, and also attended church and Sunday school classes in a local African Methodist Episcopal Church.

    Name this adventurous writer, his foster mother, and titles of two of his greatest adventure novels.

7. In 1948, the same year that he won a close election against Thomas Dewey, and running under the slogan of a "Fair Deal," this 33rd President of the U.S. issued Executive Order 9801 for the purpose of ending segregation and discrimination in the Armed Services.

   As President he had become fully aware of the patriotism, heroism and sacrifice of African American military personnel during WWII and who now deserved to be treated fairly as citizens and veterans as any American.

   Therefore, as Commander-in-Chief, and with support from the African American community and influential politicians, he desegregated the U.S. Armed Services.

   Initially, his military desegregation policy was fiercely resisted by many southern politicians like Strom Thurmond, and some high ranking military officials from the South. Name this courageous President.

8. Name this U.S. President who, in the face of mounting resistance from Southern politicians known as "Dixiecrats," courageously and skillfully used his political power to gain passage of the following landmark legislation granting African Americans first class citizenship rights:

   a. 24th Amendment in 1964 abolishing poll taxes.

   b. Civil Rights Act of 1964.

   c. Voting Rights Act of 1965.

9. In the spring of 1909, after six expeditions and seventeen attempts, Rear Admiral Robert E. Perry and his field assistant, an African American, successfully reached the North Pole.

   But it is now known that Perry's assistant actually reached the Pole and placed an American flag there before Perry.

   What is the name of Perry's assistant and what are some little known facts about his being ignored for his accomplishment, which was, in many ways, equal to Perry's?

10. In 1962, when the new head football coach was hired at Southern Methodist University in Dallas, Texas, one of the conditions in his contract that he insisted on was to be free to recruit the best players for his Mustangs' team.

Several years latter, in the face of many objections, he recruited and arranged for an athletic scholarship to be given to the first African American football player in the school's history. The player was also an academic honor student. He was from Beaumont, Texas.

For his first three years as wide receiver and punt return specialist for SMU, this 155 pound star athlete set records for himself and the school, all the while enduring racial slurs, harassment and dirty tricks from some opposing players and fans.

During this time SMU went to three bowl games, even winning over the favorite Oklahoma Sooners in the TexasBluebonnet Bowl in 1968.

This SMU coach received many honors and awards for his 37 years of football leadership. In 2004 the star player he recruited was inducted into the National College Football Hall of Fame. What is the name of this courageous coach and outstanding player?

QUIZ 35

"Black Culture" and "Ebonics": Myths and Facts

1. When did African American or "Black" culture began to emerge in the U.S., and what are some of the ways it has been expressed?

2. For many centuries, what were some of the main characteristics of slave culture?

3. What are some aspects of the dominant American secular culture that seem to have an overwhelming influence on many African American youth?

4. List five contemporary cultural values of the majority of African American families as identified by some scholars.

5. In 21st-century America, what institutions under the control of African Americans themselves seem to have an important influence on defining their reality, affirming their beliefs and values, and giving direction to their individual and group aspirations and goals?

6. What is a meaningful definition of "Black Language," "Black English," or "Ebonics," and what is the nature of its origin, development and function for African Americans?

7. What were the basic meanings of the terms, "Black Power," and "Black is Beautiful," and what non-verbal symbols were used to express them during the 1970-80s? Also, what were some critical reactions to these expressions?

8. Name ten common words or terms used by many Americans that have their origin in African and African American language dialects.

9. Comedy and humor have historically been important cultural expressions in African American community life, whether found in the church, home, among friends, or elsewhere.

   Name two of America's most hilarious African American woman and man senior citizen comedians of the latter part of 20th century, and two civil rights satirical comedians during the 1970-'80s.

10. Generally, what does the concept "soul" mean for most African Americans?

QUIZ 36
From Rap to Hip-Hop: "What it Is"

1. What do the terms "Rap" and "Hip-Hop" mean?

2. When did Rap and Hip-Hop begin in the U.S.? Name at least three 1970s disc jockeys who greatly helped to make this genre of music popular.

3. What are the stage name and real name of the Oakland, California, entertainer who became very popular for what kind of Rap in the 1970s?

4. Name the title and give the lyrics of the song that became exceedingly popular for Hip-Hop fans in 1979.

5. Who is now considered to be the "Grandfather" of Hip-Hop in the U.S. and why?

6. Identify the following four African American male rappers who became very wealthy Hip Hop millionaires:

a. In 1990, he starred in what Hollywood hit movie that opened up more acting roles for him in both movies and television?

b. In the late 1990s, this Hip-Hopper's stylistic rap performances earned him a Grammy Award and a successful acting career in what television sitcom?

c. Name a West Coast rapper and his Hip Hop album that became number one in the late 1990s.

d. During the 2004 U.S. presidential pre-election, this prominent Hip-Hop star organized a "Vote or Die" campaign. As a talented performer, Broadway actor, business executive, and record producer, he is one of America's wealthiest and most influential persons. Who is he?

7. In 2002, what multitalented talk show host, television star, and African American female rapper, whose Arabic name means both "sensitive" and "delicate," was nominated for an Oscar for her role in what movie?

8. Name two white American Hip-Hop entertainers, one female and one male, who are currently greatly admired by their followers in the U.S. One recently released a new song, "Mosh," and does the "homie dance."

9. Who were the two well-known U.S. Rap and Hip-Hop stars who were tragically shot and killed because of an unresolved personal feud between the two of them and some of their followers?

10. What is the meaning of the following Hip-Hop terms?
    a. bling-bling
    b. cabbage patch
    c. dis
    d. Djing
    e. hizzle
    f. playa hata
    g. shorty
    h. street cred
    i. tizzle
    j. wack

QUIZ 37
2002 U.S. Census Bureau Data and Other Statistical Information About African Americans

1. What is the total population of African Americans in the U.S., and what percent is this of the total U.S. population?

2. What five states in the US have the largest population of African Americans?

3. What five cities in the U.S. have the largest population of African Americans?

4. What five states have the highest percentage of African Americans as a part of their total populations?

5. What percent of the total African American population, fifteen years and older, is married, divorced and widowed?

6. What was the total number of "black-white" married couples in the U.S.: less than 250,000, nearly 300,000, or more than 350,000?

7. What percent of African American family households were maintained by a married couple, a single mother, and a single father?

8. a. Compared to the 84.1% all persons in U.S. who have attained 4 years high school education or more, what percent of African Americans have completed high school, and what percent college?
   b. How do these figures compare with the percent of African American men, 17 years and older, who are in jail or prison?

9. According to 2002 U.S. Census, the median family income for African Americans was which of the following amounts?
   a. $27,311
   b. $33,598
   c. $34,616

10. According to 2002 Bureau of Labor statistics, how many African American men and women were working in the civilian work force, and what was the unemployment rate for African Americans compared to the total population?

PART TWO:

QUIZ ANSWERS

1. In 1959-'60, two British scientists, Mary and Louis Leakey (paleoanthropoligists), discovered two-million-year-old fossil remains of extinct early human ancestors (*Zinjanthropus hominid*), in the Olduvai Gorge located in Tanzania, East Africa.

   Thirty years later, in 1990, two American scientists, Don Johanson and Tim White, reaffirmed that the earlier female fossil remains of a humanoid who was named "Lucy," found in Ethiopia's Hadar region of East Africa, is in fact some three million years old.

2. There are more than 250 different ethnic tribal groups, ranging in population size from a few thousand to millions. For example, the Dogon in Mali in West Africa have a population of over two hundred thousand, and the Zulus in South Africa have a population of millions. Other sizable groups are the Ashanti, Baganda, Bambara, Berbers, Congo, Fulani, Kikuyu, Kadisan, Lele, Mandingo, Masai, Shona, Soninke, Sotho, Wodaabe, Wolof and Yoruba.

Many of these tribal groups are quite diverse culturally. They have different languages, traditions, religions, family structures, systems of education and different levels of technological development and economic growth.

Today, however, in spite of the legacy of European colonialism, many of Africa's traditional tribal cultures are being transformed into new democratic, technological, urban and globally connected societies.

3. Long before Europeans had contact with Africans living in West Africa, there were three well-established nation-kingdoms:

Located on the coastal regions of West Africa known as the "Sudan," (an Arabic word meaning land of the blacks), the first great kingdom was Ghana (about 300-1100). It reached its peak during the reign of King Tenkamenin whose leadership brought increased trade, prosperity, law and order, and a large military build-up.

A second great kingdom and civilization was Mali. It began to emerge in 600 into a powerful, wealthy and eventually Islamic religious kingdom under the rule of Kankan Mussa or Ganga Mussa in the 1330s.

Under his rule the land area of the kingdom increased in size to include territories that are now the countries of Senegal, Gambia, Upper Volta, and part of Nigeria. With the increasing influence of Arab Islamic invaders and traders, the kingdom of Mali became very wealthy, with gold becoming one of its greatest resources.

After King Mussa's spectacular religious pilgrimage to Mecca on which he took millions of dollars worth or gold and thousands of persons in his entourage, he funded and arranged to have Arab Muslim scholars return to Mali to develop the University of

Sankore at Timbuktu.

The third and last great nation and ruler of West Africa during this time was the Islamic kingdom of Songhay. Under the rule of Askia Mohammad (1493-1529) the kingdom expanded to the south by conquering the tribal territories of Benin and Mossi.

Besides maintaining a powerful army and navy, Askia, like Mussa of Mali, directed resources into the University of Sankore at Timbuktu. It became one of the most important learning centers in Africa at that time, so much so that it attracted students and scholars from Europe, the Middle East, and other parts of Africa.

4. Throughout Africa there were well-organized systems of law and order administered by tribal leaders, based on a jury system usually composed of elders who had the consent of the tribe. These systems varied according to tribe, with morality and ethics based on traditional religious beliefs. However, in African Muslim tribal territories, laws of justice and punishment were based on the "Shariah," the legal interpretation of the Qur'an scriptures.

5. Using wood, ivory, metal, and other natural materials, African artists symbolically sculpted various images of ancestors and spirits with whom they believed they were communicating.

   Africans also made use of drums, flutes, bells, and other kinds of instruments to express a complexity of abstract and practical ideas, as well as emotional feelings.

   It is now known by language scholars that many African languages and dialects of the past, as well as the present, are very sophisticated communication systems, and have more complex grammatical structures, nuances and subleties of meaning than in some European languages.

6. Pablo Picasso (1881-1973), world-renowned Spanish painter and sculptor, acknowledged that he patterned some of his cubistic art work after African art forms.

7. The occupational skills of Africans taken into slavery were quite varied. Some came from settled agricultural villages where farming and herding of animals was the main economic activity and depended on adequate knowledge and skills.

Other slaves came from coastal villages where skills related to boating and fishing were of primary importance to those communities.

A brief list of other skills and abilities various slaves had would indicate that they were blacksmiths, brick masons, carpenters, herbalists, iron and gold metallurgists, midwives, weavers, woodcarvers, and so forth.

8. Africans taken into slavery came from different religious backgrounds. Some followed ancient traditional monotheistic and polytheistic religions. Many slaves were Muslims whose families had been members of the religion for many generations. A much smaller number were Jews and Christians.

As with any civilized group of people, the religions of African slaves were very meaningful, ethical, and spiritually fulfilling for the individual and the tribe.

9. The vast majority of slaves were taken from the coastal areas of West Africa, often referred to as being a part of Black Africa or the Sudan. It encompassed the present-day countries of Gambia, Sierra Leone, Ivory Coast, Ghana, Benin, Nigeria and Cameroon. A lesser number of slaves were also taken from the Congo region of West-Central Africa and parts of East Africa, depending on the access and economic motivation of slave traders.

10. The continent of Africa has an area of 11,717,370 square miles; the U.S. has 3,794,085 square miles, Europe 8,868,680 square miles, and Asia has 12,312,740 square miles.

EBONY OWL'S: DID YOU KNOW?

Contrary to the many negative stereotypes of the past that Africans were "wild and wooly," uncivilized savages, and people with limited intelligence and achievement, it is now recognized by 21st-century scholars that Africans are the ancestors of all humans, and that past civilizations of Africans have provided a cultural and technological foundation from which all human civilizations have evolved.

Tragically, to counteract the many centuries that Africans have suffered from slavery, racism, colonialism, internal strife, and genocide, and currently from AIDS and other diseases, it will require massive international assistance and reparations before Africans are able to arrive at their full potential in the 21st century.

Working in concert with Africans, the people of America can play an important role in helping to bring about their economic progress, and governmental stability.

Africa, too, in the near and distant future can greatly benefit the world with its vast human and natural resources. This will depend largely, of course, on the peaceful resolution of its very serious internal ethnic, economic and political problems.

1. Attila, the Hun. According to Chinese 5th-century C.E. annals, Attila was a Mongol leader of African ancestry whose victorious armies conquered many people and lands in China and parts of the Roman Empire in the West.

2. Alexander Dumas. He was born in 1802 in the small island country of Haiti. His mother was of African ancestry, and his father was part French and African, and held the rank of general in the Haitian army.

   Dumas, the writer, left Haiti and went to live in France where he completed writing and publishing both "The Three Musketeers" and "The Count of Monte Cristo" in the 1840s.

3. The Queen of Sheba, an Ethiopian ruler, is mentioned both in the Bible (Song of Solomon 1:5), and in the Qur'an (Surah XXVII).

4. Cleopatra, Queen of Egypt, 69-3 B.C.E., and Rome's great emperor, Julius Caesar, fell passionately in love with each other, even though their romantic affair was against the traditional customs of their respective countries. Cleopatra gave birth to Caesar's son, who was named Caesarion in honor of his father, Caesar.

   After Caesar's assassination in Rome, Mark Antony, his successor, was also captivated by Cleopatra's beauty, charm and intelligence. He left Rome and his right to rule, and went to Egypt to live and jointly rule with Cleopatra. During the thirteen years they were together they had three children: Alexander Helios, Ptolemy and Cleopatra Silene.

5. As military leader of the Theban Legion he was known as Maurice. But after he refused to go to war against Christians, because he himself was a recent Christian convert, he was executed by the Romans and eventually became a Church martyr.

   Later he received sainthood as St. Moritz or St. Maurice, and in 1230, eastern German Catholics dedicated their cathedral at Magdeburg in honor of him.

6. His African name was Olaudah Equiano before he was captured and sold into slavery as a boy. As an adult he became known as Gustavus Vassa in both Virginia and England, and while in England he made a plea to Queen Charlotte in 1775 to emancipate slaves. The title of his slave narrative was, "The Interesting Narrative of the Life of Olaudah Equiano, or Gustavus the African."

7. Queen Charlotte Sophia (1744-1818), wife of England's George III. The large megalopolis city of Charlotte in North Carolina, Charlottesville, Virginia, and Charlottetown of Prince Edward Island in Canada, were all named after the Queen when they were first settled. She also became an advocate for abolishing slavery.

8. Toussaint L'Ouverture was one of thousands of African slaves whose labors were exploited by the French colonists in Saint Dominque during most of the 1700s.

   However, Toussaint's military ability, his astuteness, and perhaps his charisma associated with his small stature, enabled him to lead a successful grassroots insurrection and revolution against the French in 1801. Haiti thus became the second independent nation in the Americas after the U.S.

9. According to local history and traditional celebrations in the small town of Yanga, Mexico, an enslaved African prince was taken from the Ivory Coast in the early 1600s by Spanish slavers. After he escaped his captors, he led a successful armed revolt to win freedom for himself and other enslaved Africans and Native Americans in that area. The town of Yanga bears his name.

10. Alexander Sergeyevich Pushkin (1799-1837). In the early 1800s, he became one of Russia's leading poets and novelists, writing such poetic works as "Boris Gudinov," and great novels like "The Bronze Horseman" and "The Captain's Daughter."

The historical significance of African and African American achievements and contributions to human culture and progress, and especially for America, is yet to be fully known and given credible recognition.

An excellent source fulfilling this lack of credible information is James M. Brodie's book, "Created Equal: The Lives and Ideas of Black American Innovators." It provides a wealth of unknown factual information about the creative and ingenious cultural and technological talents of African American people.

A similar book focusing on the remarkable accomplishments of contemporary African Americans is Dick Russell's anthology, "Black Genius."

And finally, J.A. Roger's pioneering and classic book, "World's Great Men of Color," is a vital reading for everyone who wants a broader knowledge of the contributions of persons of African ancestry.

QUIZ 3 ANSWERS

African and African American Diaspora and Migration

1. According to the findings of an international team of scientists, especially Li Jin, a leading Chinese geneticist, it has now been determined that some of the genetic ancestors of the people of China came from Africa.

   His evidence indicates that the migration of some peoples from Africa to China, and to other parts of Asia, involved a complex pattern of migration that took place many thousands of years ago. These findings were presented as part of the Chinese Human Diversity Project publication in the "Proceedings of the National Academy of Sciences" in 1998.

2. Some modern ethnologists have concluded that the dark-complexioned Dravidians of South India and the Tamils of Sri Lanka have ancient African ancestors.

3. Hannibal was a great military leader from the city-state of Carthage in North Africa. In the 2nd Punic War he led his elephant-riding army through Europe's rugged Alps Mountains to wage war and establish strongholds in Italy.

4. In the 1980s, a number of Olmec artifacts were determined to show images of people with distinctive African physical features.

5. Spain and Portugal, because of their earlier explorations of West African coastal areas, and their increasing need for cheap labor to build and develop their colonial settlements and plantation investments in the New World.

   From 1450 to 1600, it is estimated that thousands of Africans were also taken to Spain to work as slaves. After conversion to the Catholic religion, some were eventually assimilated into Spanish society as full citizens.

6. In the early 1600s, English colonists in Virginia began to prosper increasingly from their labor-intensive tobacco plantations and exports to Europe. But they found that the use of Native American and European white indentured servant labor was not as productive and profitable as African slave labor.

Eventually, they found that buying and investing in African slaves would bring them greater profits, and provide them with valuable capital resources and economic wealth.

Investments in slaves were considered to be one of the best financial investments at the time, with good potential returns just as certain stock market investments in biotechnology research companies are thought to be profitable in the 21st century.

As a matter of fact, the paper currency of some Confederate states had engraved images of African American slaves, portraying them as happily and willingly working on farms and performing other kinds of labor, thereby, visually conveying the idea that investing in the slave-based economy of the South was a good thing for all concerned.

7. For many decades, most of the African slaves brought to the North American English mainland colonies were first taken to island colonies. In such places as Barbados and Jamaica, various methods were used to physically and psychologically force new slaves to conform to the lifestyle and occupational demands of slave life. Once this process was considered complete, the "seasoned" slave would be sold on the slave market, especially to mainland slavers.

8. After the Revolutionary War, thousands of Africans, free and slave, who fought for and gave support to the British, felt compelled to leave the rebellious American colonies and flee to Canada and other places for fear of retaliation from the victorious Americans.

   For being loyal, the British fulfilled their promise to give these "loyalists" parcels of land in Nova Scotia, Canada, and today, a sizeable population of the descendents of this group live in Preston, Nova Scotia.

9. In 1815, with the backing of a wealthy free African American sea captain, Paul Cuff, and sailing on one of his ships, a group of 38 African Americans were the first to emigrate from the U.S..

   They sailed to Sierra Leone, a British colony where some freed African slaves had already settled, including some émigrés from Nova Scotia. They wanted to establish their own country and be free from slavery.

10. During and after the Civil War, thousands of African Americans migrated northward and westward from the South in order to get away from the many forms of brutal racial oppression and violent hostility they were forced to experience every day. They also wanted to take advantage of the federal government's land-grant program passed in 1862. It granted up to 160 acres of designated free land to those who were eligible to settle and farm on it according to certain guidelines.

    Many also migrated and settled in Kansas, Arkansas, Missouri, and Nebraska, for economic reasons as well as to avoid racism.

    In the 20th century, especially during and after World Wars I and II, many African Americans migrated into the northeastern and western U.S. to seek employment, and to have freer and better living conditions than in the South.

Some writers estimate that after the Civil War, more than 60,000 African Americans migrated from the South into nearby non-slave states such as Kansas and established their own communities.

For example, Nicodemus, an all-black town that was founded by African American migrants in northwestern Kansas after the Civil War, eventually grew to have a population of more than 20,000.

It is estimated that hundreds of thousands of African Americans migrated from the South to the northeastern and western states during World Wars I and II in order to get work in war-related manufacturing industries, assembly plants, meat packing plants, and the railroads. They also wanted to obtain greater freedom and a better life for themselves and their children.

Today, there seems to be a "Back to the South" migration movement on the part of many younger generation African Americans who believe they can obtain better economic opportunities and quality of life in that region of the country than elsewhere.

QUIZ 4 ANSWERS

African People's Active Participation in Spanish, French, Dutch and English Colonies in North America

1. The African Spaniard, Estevanico (Little Stephen) was a slave servant and member of Panfilo de Narvaez's expedition to North America in the early 1500s.

   After several years of travel, mapping and exploration into the southwestern region of the future U.S., Estevanico's ability to translate some southwest Native American Indian tribal languages became a valuable asset for later Spanish conquest and colonization of the area.

2. York was William Clark's African American slave valet (body servant). He is referred to in Clark's journal as being a scout and doing some trading for the expedition, especially with some Native American tribes the group encountered during their journey.

   There is no clear uncontroversial evidence that York ever received any compensation for his service during the expedition, or that he got his freedom and was manumitted by Clark.

3. Jean-Baptiste Pointe DuSable was born in Haiti and educated in Paris by Jesuit Catholics, and came to North America as a member of a French exploration group into the Great Lakes area of North America.

Later, he established a very small trading center near the mouth of the Chicago River with the help of his wife, a Potawatomi Indian, who is credited with helping him to run the business and make it quite successful.

Today, in the city of Chicago, an excellent well-established museum focuses on the life of DuSable and the importance of his trading center becoming the nucleus for the future city.

4.   In the Dutch colony of New Netherlands, slaves were often hired out by their owners to work as blacksmiths, carpenters, chimneysweepers, coopers, longshoremen, domestics, and other manual workers.

The owners received most of the money from the slave's labor, and the slave got the remainder. As a result, slaves who worked on this basis had more freedom, and more opportunities to earn some money for themselves, and therefore could eventually save enough to buy their freedom, and that of other family members. This was not the case in most of the colonies where slaves were restricted to work mainly on plantations doing agricultural work, and usually for no money compensation.

5.   Early colonial records indicate that the first group of Africans to settle in Virginia arrived on a Dutch ship in 1619 as indentured servants. For several decades, they had rights and a social status similar to white indentured servants who lived there, but this began to change in the 1660s because of emerging discriminatory racist and religious laws.

6. In 1624, a child named William Tucker was baptized in Jamestown, Virginia. His parents, Isabella and Antonio, are listed among the first settlers of Jamestown.

7. Abraham Pearce who came from the West Indies and settled in the Pilgrims' colony in Plymouth, Massachusetts, as early as 1623. Plymouth colonial records indicate that he was a free person, a farmer and a voting member of the settlement.

   He also married one of the women in the colony and they had five children. It wasn't until 1643 that his race was mentioned in the colony's record as "Abraham Pearce, blackamore."

8. They worked as blacksmiths, brick masons, carpenters, chimneysweepers, cooks, coachmen, horse groomers, house servants, longshoremen, and nannies, etc.

   It has now been documented that slaves did much of the physical and skilled work building and maintaining George Washington's Mount Vernon estate, Thomas Jefferson's Monticello estate, the U.S. Capitol, and other federal facilities in Washington, D.C. Slaves also did much of the construction work for some state and local levels of government.

9. By the mid-1700s Maryland had an estimated 43,450 slaves and 97,623 whites. Virginia had 101,452 slaves and 129,581 whites. These colonies had large slave populations mainly because of the investment and use of slaves to make profits from their tobacco plantations.

   However, Georgia had a slave population of only 1,000, and 4,200 whites. This was because of the many English poor whites and debtors who were compelled to immigrate to the colony in the 1730s, and they provided cheap labor for the Georgia colonial economy rather than African slaves.

   It wasn't until after 1750 that many more African slaves were brought into the colony to work on the increasing number of cotton plantations being established.

10. By 1850 it is estimated that Portugal had forcibly transported the largest number of African slaves to its New World colony of Brazil, estimated to be about 5 million. France brought the least number of slaves to the New World, and mostly to their colony of Haiti.

From the 1500s-1850s, European conquest and colonization of Africa, and the increasing enslavement and use of African slaves, brought great prosperity to the political and economic interests who controlled these movements. Ultimately it created a capital wealth source that became the foundation for further economic progress and development in the U.S. and other parts of the world, even up to the present.

On the other hand, it depleted the African continent of its most valuable human resources, its potential for progress, its economic and political stability, and the necessary basis for meeting the needs of its people. It is a sad and tragic commentary that continues to challenge all of humanity in the 21st century.

1. In 1790, the first U.S. census recorded a total population estimate of 4 million, including 757,000 slaves and 60,000 "free persons." At the time, African Americans, including both slave and quasi-free, represented about 20% or one-fifth of the total U.S. population.

2. a. The "Three-Fifths Compromise" implication in Article I, Section 2 of the U.S. Constitution read: "Representatives and direct taxes shall be apportioned among the several States which may be included within this Union, according to their respective Numbers, which shall be determined by adding to the whole Number of the free Persons, including those bound to Service for a Term of Years, and excluding Indians not taxed, three fifths of all other persons."

   This article in the Constitution gave states with slave populations the right to count their slaves on the basis of a three-fifths numerical fraction when determining that state's representation in Congress, and its federal taxes on the same three-fifths basis. This compromise helped to resolve a critical political issue between southern states that had large slave populations, and northern states that had much smaller populations.

b. Cessation of Slave Importation in Article I, Section 9, Clause 1 reads: "The Migration or Importation of such Persons as any of the States now existing shall think proper to admit, shall not be prohibited by the Congress prior to the Year one thousand eight hundred and eight, but a Tax or duty may be imposed on such importation, not exceeding ten dollars for each Person."

Although the Constitution prohibited slave importation beginning in 1808, it is estimated that perhaps 300,000 more African slaves had been smuggled into the U.S. after this date up until 1859. In this year, the *Clothilde,* is recorded to have been one of the last ships bringing slaves to a U.S. port in Alabama.

c. The Constitutional Status of Runaway Slaves in Article IV, Section 2, Clause 3 stated: "No person held to Service or Labour in one State, under the laws thereof, escaping into another, shall, in consequence of any Law or Regulation therein, be discharged from such Service of Labour, but shall be delivered up on Claim of the Party to whom such Service or Labour may be due."

This article essentially required that all runaway slaves must be returned to the rightful owner who claimed them, regardless of any legal challenges by the slave.

3. African American slaves were essentially defined as "property." They were specifically considered the "chattel" or personal property of the owner. Hence, they were legally under the control and utilization of the owner for life unless the slave was sold or "manumitted" (set free) in some other way by the owner.

4. Many scholars use the term "quasi-free" to refer to those African Americans who were by law free persons, but whose free status did not guarantee them the same rights and privileges as a free white person. Quasi-free African Americans were often treated quite differently compared to white persons. They were subject to arbitrary decisions regarding their rights and what they could do and not do when interacting with whites. They were also at the risk of being forced back into slavery by unscrupulous persons.

5. "Manumission" was a term used to refer to a slave who could obtain his or her freedom, usually by one of the following ways up until the end of the Civil War:

a. Buying one's freedom based on an amount determined by a willing owner or by a proxy.

b. At the time of the owner's death, a formally recognized will of the owner or beneficiary could grant freedom to a slave or to a slave family.

c. Statutory law in some states. Under some circumstances becoming a Christian convert, especially for some who were born and baptized as a Catholic Christian.

6. An average of 600-800 dollars was paid for a healthy and potentially productive male slave 20 to 40 years old, and a comparable amount for a young female of childbearing age. The equivalent value today (2006) in the U.S. would be approximately twelve to fifteen thousand dollars.

7. Vermont abolished slavery in 1777, Pennsylvania in 1780, Massachusetts in 1783, Rhode Island and Connecticut in 1784. These states abolished slavery mainly in response to the growing influence of the abolitionists demanding an end to slavery, and also as a reward to those slaves who had fought in the Revolutionary War against the British.

8. Dred Scott was a slave born in Virginia in 1795, and then bought by different owners until he ended up in Missouri, a slave state.

    From Missouri he was taken to work and reside in the non-slave state of Illinois and to an area that is now Fort Snelling, Minnesota, located near the Twin Cities.

    When he was brought back to Missouri, he was encouraged by abolitionists to sue his owner for his freedom, and to argue in the courts that since he had lived in non-slave parts of the country he was therefore a "free" person.

    Nevertheless, when the US. Supreme Court eventually heard his case, they ruled that since he was "chattel" slave property (legally owned by someone), he had no legal right under the Constitution to sue for his freedom because he was not a citizen of the U.S.

9. In 1860, cotton, rice, and indigo were the main crops grown in the South because they brought large profits, especially cotton, which was a big export crop to England.

   Consequently, to maximize profits, and also meet the demand for the cheapest source of labor, plantation owners procured more and more slaves.

   Also, many slaves brought their African rice growing skills to the colonies long before being compelled to grow cotton and indigo in the colonies.

10. For the year 1850 alone, historical economists Robert W. Fogel and Stanley L. Engerman estimated that African American slave workers suffered a monetary loss in wages and other benefits that add up to an amount of 84 million dollars.

EBONY OWL" DID YOU KNOW?

Between 1787 - 1865 the institution of slavery in America had become an inseparable part of the nation's economic growth and prosperity, especially in the South.

Fueld by the demands for cotton in both Europe and the U.S., and Eli Whitney's "cotton gin" speeding up the production of cotton, the relative "cheap and free" slave labor became indespensible to the whole system.

According to Broadus N. Butler, "Free and slave Blacks made contributions to economic development as mechanics, artisans, craftsmen, shipbuilders and sail makers, shoe and clothing makers, brick and lumber manufacturers, furniture and cabinetmakers, wrought iron and silver crafters, ... "

Hence, it must be understood that African American slaves played a crucial role in bringing immense profits to those in power who controlled the government and economic interests at the time.

As in the 21st century, there are those who place more value on material and money interests than on human rights, and social justice.

QUIZ 6 ANSWERS

*Freedom Fighters, Patriots and Heroes
in the American Revolution
and War of Independence*

1. Crispus Attucks, a forty-seven year old seaman and former slave, and four other Massachusetts colonists were shot and killed by British soldiers on the eve of the American Revolutionary War.

   Today, in the city's historic park, Boston Commons, there is a life-size statute of Attucks and the others commemorating their heroism and martyrdom.

---

2. Peter Salem and Salem Poor. Peter Salem, although a slave, fought with a group of Colonial "Minutemen" under Captain Simon Edgel. In a crucial battle at Bunker Hill overlooking Boston, Peter fired a shot from his musket that mortally wounded British Major Pitcairn. This became a favorable turning point in the war and an important victory for the Americans. Salem became an instant hero, and after the war was given a monetary reward and his freedom.

Salem Poor, on the other hand, was a free African American who also joined the Minutemen in the colonists' war against the British. Like Peter Salem, he too, is credited with having shot to death a British officer at Bunker Hill, by the rank and name of Lt. Colonel James Ambercrombie. Salem Poor's commanding officer, Colonel William Prescott, and thirteen other Colonial army officers signed a formal petition citing and commending him for his distinguished service.

3. Prince Whipple and Oliver Cromwell. Whipple was an African slave who had become the personal bodyguard and valet for General William Whipple of New Hampshire, who was his legal owner. Whipple wore a distinctive turban and because of this it is believed by some historians that he was son of an African Muslim king, and a previous victim of European slavers.

Oliver Cromwell was a free African American farmer who enlisted in the Second New Jersey Regiment to fight against the British. He fought in a number of battles, and after the war was awarded the Badge of Merit and a discharge signed by General George Washington. He was also given an annual federal pension of $96.00 a year for his military service during the war.

4. William Lee was George Washington's lifelong devoted slave companion and valet, who accompanied him throughout the Revolutionary war. After the war, Washington gave Lee his freedom and provided money for him to be taken care of in his old age.

5. When slave James Armistead wandered about in the British army camps during the Revolutionary war, he was hardly suspected of gathering very detailed information about their troop numbers and military status.

The British apparently thought he was someone's dumb and dutiful slave, not recognizing that his antics were a cover-up for his spying activities.

In fact, he was spying for the young, twenty-year-old French commanding officer, Major General Lafayette. His French troops were fighting along with

the Americans in the war against the British, and he gave Armistead the assignment.

After the war, Lafayette wrote a certificate describing in detail Armistead's courageous and heroic efforts that helped the French and the Americans defeat the British.

When the war was over, Armistead was granted his freedom

and a yearly pension of $40.00 from the Virginia General Assembly, and he and Lafayette remained lifelong friends, which greatly influenced Armistead to change his last name to "Lafayette."

6. The "Bucks of America" was the only all-African American company of volunteer soldiers to fight in the Revolutionary War. Colonel Middleton was the "Bucks" commander, the only African American commanding officer during the war.

   Near the close of the war, one of America's founding fathers and signers of the Declaration of Independence, John Hancock, presented the Bucks with their own company flag and cited them for their bravery and heroism.

7. Fontages Legion was made up of 500-700 Haitian African soldiers who were a fighting unit under the command of the French Army, who were allies with the Americans. The Legion fought courageously to help defeat the British in battles at Savannah, Georgia.

8. a. Deborah Gannett who served with the Fourth Massachusetts Regiment. She disguised herself as a man and enlisted under the name of "Robert Shurtliff." After the war she was commended by the state legislature for her outstanding service and given money for her time of service.

b. Phobe Fraunces was the daughter of Samuel Fraunces, a.k.a. "Black Sam," a well-known restaurant owner of Fraunces Tavern located in New York's Manhattan. Before and during the Revolutionary war it was a favorite place for well-known celebrities to meet and enjoy good food. It was formerly known as "Queen's Head" and was named after Queen Charlotte of England. It became a popular meeting place for George Washington and some of his close friends and associates.

Phobe learned that one of Washington's bodyguards, Sergeant Thomas Hickey, had entered into a secret plan with the British to poison Washington's food when he came to the tavern.

Learning of this from Hickey, who fancied her, Phobe told her father, who forewarned Washington.

The plot was foiled, Hickey was arrested, tried, convicted, and afterwards was hung before a crowd of some 20,000 onlookers in New York City.

9. Austin Dabney is one of the little known African American freedom fighters. His master was drafted, but instead of going to war himself, he sent his slave Dabney whom he promised to free for doing so.

After the war, Dabney was not only given his freedom but was officially commended by the Governor of Georgia for his bravery and courage, and was granted some 100 acres of land as well as a pension.

10. Estimates of 5 to 8 thousand fought on the side of the American colonists against the British, and some 10 to 20 thousand for the British.

EBONY OWL: DID YOU KNOW?

One of the main motivations for African slaves fighting on either side during the Revolutionary War was the promise of receiving "manumission" or freedom from slavery. Some were actually fighting in the place of their masters. However, those African Americans who were free persons fought primarily as patriots, and like other Americans were also fighting for freedom from British colonialism, and for the freedom of their slave brothers and sisters.

It is ironic that some six months after Gen-

eral Washington's taking command of the Continental Army in July of 1775, and his initial refusal to allow any African American men to serve in the army, he was compelled to reverse that decision and allow African American men to fight with the Continental Army.

There were two main reasons for his decision. First, the Continental Army was not successful in recruiting and retaining the number of white troops they had anticipated, and second the British had already recruited slaves and other quasi-free African Americans to fight with them and as a reward receive manumission. This greatly increased their military assets and put Washington's army at a great manpower disadvantage.

1. It wasn't until 1821 that a group of 80 free African Americans established a settlement on the Atlantic coast of West Africa. It was located at Cape Mesurado about 80 miles south of Sierra Leone's border.

2. The main motivation of this group was to spread Christianity and to find a place of repatriation where African Americans and other African people would be free from slavery, and join together to establish a country of their own.

   The American Colonization Society was made up of a number of influential and well-off white southern Americans. They raised thousands of dollars from religious organizations and philanthropists to support this new African American colony.

3. Two Virginian Congressmen, Henry Clay, Speaker of the House, and John Rankin of Roanoke, as well as U.S. President James Monroe, were all instrumental in supporting the movement.

As a result of their influence, in 1821, Congress was persuaded and approved $100,000 in government money and military support to assist the colonization effort. Funds were channeled through the American Colonization Society (ACS) which was supported by a number of Christian Churches.

4. In 1847, Joseph J. Jenkins of Virginia became the first non-white governor. He was an African American who had immigrated to the colony in 1829. In consultation with others he officially had the colony named the "Free and Independent Republic of Liberia." The new nation's name, "Liberia" was taken from the Latin word *liber* meaning free. "Monrovia" was the name given to the capitol city to honor U.S. President James Monroe.

5. Liberia consists of 37,743 sq. miles and is comparable in land size to the state of Tennessee. However, its geography and climate is quite different. Liberia is mostly a plateau with an annual rainfall of more than 150 inches along the coastal areas and about half that amount in inland areas. The land and the climate are ideal for growing such crops as bananas, coffee, cocoa, rice, sugarcane, palm oil, and rubber.

6. The current population of the Republic of Liberia is estimated to be 3,367,000.

    "Americo-Liberian" is the name given to the approximate 3% of Liberians who are the descendents of the original African American settlers. They were the dominant political group in the country for many decades until 1971. Although English is the official language and is taught in the schools, Mande, Kwa, and West Atlantic tribal languages are also spoken in some areas.

    The Kpelle, Bassa, and Grebo are the largest indigenous ethnic tribal groups.

7. Liberia has a form of federal government patterned after the United States. Its official name is the "Republic of Liberia" with a 26 member Senate and 64 member House of Representatives. It was the first republic established on the continent of Africa. For many decades the official currency of Liberia was based on the U.S. dollar and monetary system.

8. 63% or the majority of the population follow traditional African religious beliefs and practices, 21% are Christian, and 16% Muslim.

9. William V.S. Tubman, an Americo-Liberian descendent, was elected president of the republic in 1944 and served nearly six terms. Since his death in 1971, there has been considerable instability in governmental affairs for more than thirty years.

10. Charles Taylor, an ex-convict, was questionably elected in 1997. However, in 2003, rebels forced him to resign, and subsequently a United Nations tribunal indicted him for being involved in war crimes involving Sierra Leone.

Today, after 14 years of almost continuous civil war and instability, Liberian citizens, under United Nations support and protection, has elected its first president in an atmosphere of free elections.

In November, 2005, Mrs. Ellen Johnson-Sirleaf was elected President of Liberia. She is the first woman ever to be elected president of a nation in Africa.

Some African experts make the charge that in the 21st century the U.S. has done very little economically or politically to bolster the Republic of Liberia, compared to U.S. involvement and alliances with countries in other parts of the world, especially the Middle East.

Since 1949, the nation of Liberia has legally held U.S.-based shipping registry rights. This allows the nation of Liberia the right to issue U.S. Ship registration certificates to ships meeting certain criteria and as a result earn some economic gain.

Currently, Liberia hosts more than 2,000 foreign vessels, offering them low fees, and allowing some shippers to meet what they would consider to be "easy" regulations.

Also, about one-third of U.S. oil imports arrive with Liberian flagged tankers.

Nevertheless, Liberia's overall future economic and political progress is in great need of proactive U.S. support and partnership.

QUIZ 8 ANSWERS

Runaway Slaves and the Underground Freedom Train

1. It was a term that probably began with the slaves themselves to refer to secret escape routes, and it also became known as the "freedom train."

   Fugitive slaves and their secret supporters cleverly used such code words as: "conductors"= abolitionists who helped them escape; "passenger"= runaway slave; and "station" and "depot"= safe hiding places. It enabled them to talk about their activities without being readily detected.

2. The slave runaway provision of the 1781 Constitution, and the 1851 Fugitive Slave Law, caused both slaves and abolitionists to become more active in organizing and supporting U.G.R.R. activities until the end of the Civil War. This was certainly the case for some members of the Quaker religious group, now known as "Friends." They took a very active part in U.G.R.R. operations. Many of their church leaders and members supported and helped to orchestrate various kinds of activities at much risk to themselves individually and to their church groups.

3. The Underground Railroad extended northward into a number of northern states such as Maryland, Ohio, and Pennsylvania, in particular. It also went further north into Canada, and even south into Mexico.

4. At night, the slaves would usually leave their plantations and travel as many miles as they could before daybreak. They would walk and run along trails, cross rivers, ford swamps, and climb mountains seeking freedom.

    Abolitionists would provide various kinds of transportation for the runaways on specially designed wagons, carriages, ferryboats, and other conveyances where the runaways hid in secret compartments. Some abolitionists hid them and fed them in their own homes.

    Slaves used various kinds of disguises in order to escape. In some cases a male slave would feign stupidity or dress and act like a woman and therefore would not be as suspect as a runaway.

    Those who had light complexions and could "pass" for white would pretend to be the owner or master of a dark-complexioned slave in some cases.

5. a. One slave, Henry Brown, hid inside a freight box, and was safely express shipped from the slave South to some abolitionists in Philadelphia without ever being detected.

b. Another dramatic escape involved a slave couple, William and Ellen Craft, who took the role of slave mistress and slave while traveling on a train from the South to New England. Ellen, having a light complexion, portrayed herself as slave owner. Her husband, William, who was much darker, acted as though he was her obedient slave. This kind of role-playing enabled them to successfully escape.

6. Harriet Tubman (1820-1913).

7. William Still (1821-1902).

8. "Get on Board, Little Children," "Steal Away to Jesus," and "Swing Low Sweet Chariot."

9. An estimated 100,000 slaves valued at approximately 40 million dollars fled from the South traveling on the Underground Railroad.

10. First, they influenced Congress to enact the Missouri Compromise for the purpose of separating the country into existing and future slave states and non-slave states. This in effect gave approval to slavery in those states where it already existed and some new states.

Congress also passed the 1850 Fugitive Slave Law requiring runaway slaves to be returned to their masters regardless of where they were found, and punishment to those who interfered in the process.

Finally, slave owners could legally employ "bounty hunters" to travel anywhere to search for and apprehend runaway slaves.

The abolition of slavery became the nation's most widely supported social movement in American society in the 19th century prior to the Civil War. It not only focused on getting freedom for slaves, but it was also an attempt to deal with the moral issue of slavery, its fundamental rightness or wrongness, and its contradiction of basic American Constitutional ideals and rights.

One of the most powerful and clear voices for abolishing slavery was the former slave Frederick Douglass. He often spoke about slaves being given their immediate freedom, and to do otherwise would betray the nation's own basic ideals.

Speaking to a mostly all-white audience in Rochester, New York, the day after July 4th, 1852 he declared the following:

"What to the American slave is your Fourth of July? I answer, a day that reveals to him more than all other days of the year, the gross injustice and cruelty of which he is a constant victim. To him your celebration is a sham..."

QUIZ 9 ANSWERS

Institutional Slavery, Racial Segregation and Discrimination in the United States Before, During and After the Civil War

1. a. "Institutional Slavery" refers to a comprehensive structure and system of slavery that developed and existed in the U.S. for more than two-hundred years (1660s-1865). It was legally sanctioned and morally approved by most levels of government, especially in the South, and in many ways interfaced with the operation of other major institutions.

    For example, it is interesting to note that in a 2002 California Department of Insurance Report, reference was made to such large insurance companies as Aetna, Manhattan Life, and New York Insurance Company, and their past connection with slavery.

    The report brought out the fact that during the slavery era these companies were issuing policies to protect slave owners from the financial loss of their slave chattel property.

    Also, during this time, some religious institutions (Christian and Jewish) took theological positions to morally uphold and defend slavery on religious grounds. They interpreted the Bible in ways that justified slavery, and various practices of racial segregation and discrimination against slaves as well as against African Americans generally.

As a consequence, African Americans were devalued as human beings, and usually treated with incivility and hostility by most white persons in the South and in some other parts of the country as well.

b. The primary driving force for the development of institutional slavery was the economic and social gain for those who owned slaves. The slaves' labor was free and could be used to make money and a profit for the owner.

Slaves were also valuable to slave-owning families because they provided a whole range of domestic house services such as cooks, nannies, personal valets, groundskeepers, carriage drivers, garbage collectors, gardeners, handymen, and toilet and outhouse providers, etc.

The services provided by slaves inevitably enhanced the comfort and convenience level of slave owners, their families, and also the general society.

Most slaves, however, worked in arduous non-domestic service roles as field hands on farms and plantations where they worked from sun-up to sundown, tilling, planting, and harvesting crops; mainly cotton, rice, tobacco, and indigo for their owners. Many slave men labored at cutting, logging, and milling trees, and many worked as longshoremen, loading and handling various kinds of materials and products for transport to and from manufacturing and railroad centers. Others worked at river docks and seaports.

c. Since the slave was basically defined and perceived as "property," and not as a person deserving or entitled to any kind of human rights, many generations of African Americans became the victims of all kinds of damaging physical and psychological abuse associated with both institutional slavery and racism.

Both institutional slavery and white racism resulted in a separation and segregation of the races, and ultimately brought about a great racial and social divide between white and black Americans, that ultimately divided the nation and was a major underlying cause of the Civil War.

2. In 1861, there were twelve states that had laws prohibiting slavery: California, Connecticut, Illinois, Indiana, Iowa, Massachusetts, Michigan, New Jersey, New York, Ohio, Pennsylvania, and Rhode Island.

Eleven states had laws approving: Alabama, Arkansas, Florida, Georgia, Louisiana, Mississippi, North Carolina, Tennessee, Texas, and Virginia. The remaining eleven states had ambiguous policies.

3. a. Abraham Lincoln's Emancipation Proclamation, issued under his executive order in 1863, declared that slaves were free in the rebel Confederate states only.

Ironically, it did not abolish slavery in Washington, D.C., the nation's capital, nor in the nearby states of Delaware and Maryland, where slavery continued to be practiced until 1865.

b. It wasn't until the U.S. Congress passed the 13th Amendment to the Constitution, in 1865, that slavery was abolished throughout the nation. Some four million African Americans were freed, and a much smaller number of Native American Indians who had also been held as slaves.

4. a. The 14th Amendment granted citizenship to all former slaves at both the federal and state levels in 1868. And one of the immediate and practical consequences of the 14th Amendment was to require all slaves to register a full legal identity. This meant that slaves had to register both a first name and a last name or surname with the census recorder in the county or territory in which they resided.

Sometimes to expedite this process the census taker or name recorder would arbitrarily assign the freed slave a complete first and last name, and in some cases even assign a freed slave his or her owner's last name.

There are thousands of cases when freed slaves were given a "Lincoln," "Washington," or "Jefferson," last name. Prior to this, African American name identity was by first name only, and that was often given by or agreed to by the slave owner.

The slave-master conflict about name identity was vividly portrayed in the slave character of Kunta Kinte in Alex Haley's "Roots" book and movie. Kunta Kinte tried very hard to maintain his African name, but was forced by his master to take on the slave name of "Toby."

Today, the vast majority of African Americans have retained names that historically originated out of this process, names which are mostly Anglo-European in cultural origin: English, Irish, Scottish and French.

Only a very small percent of African Americans have names derived from indigenous African languages and cultures, and an even smaller number have Muslim derived names.

Most African Americans have held on to their family surnames. They have done this out of respect for their own particular meaningful family history and genealogy.

b. The Fifteenth Amendment that was passed in 1870 gave voting and political rights to African American men, but not to women. All American women did not get their voting rights until 1920 with the passage of the 19th Amendment.

This affirmative amendment to the Constitution made it possible for hundreds of African American men, mostly in the former Confederate states, to have significant political power for the first time ever in American history, and to be elected and appointed to government positions.

5. The 1866 Civil Rights Act enacted by Congress granted African Americans the following specific rights: "...to make and enforce contracts, to sue, be parties, and give evidence, to inherit, purchase, lease, sell, hold, and convey real and personal property, and to full and equal benefit of all laws and proceedings for the security of person and property, as is enjoyed by white citizens..."

Even though this federal legislation was well-intentioned by Congress, it was soon deliberately challenged, undermined and made a mockery of by southern politicians at all levels of government until the enactment of the 1964 Civil Rights legislation.

6. After the passage of the 14th and 15th Amendments, and the 1866 Civil Rights Act, lawmakers in the South began to pass a series of so-called "Black Codes" or laws enacted mainly for the purpose of preventing African Americans from exercising and benefiting from their Constitutional rights.

They provided ways to politically and extra-legally prevent African Americans from exercising their civil and constitutional rights. An example of such a law or "code" was the "grandfather clause" enacted by a number of southern state governments as a voting prerequisite. In order to vote, one's father and/or grandfather had to have been a registered voter prior to the Civil War that began in 1861, a requirement that was utterly impossible for former slaves to meet since slavery was not officially abolished until 1865.

The net effect of these laws and similar laws, such as poll taxes and literacy tests, was to effectively disfranchise practically all African Americans living in southern states for more than 100 years.

It wasn't until the passage of the Voting Rights Act of 1965 that disfranchisement laws began to be eliminated from the American political process in the South.

7. During the 1870-'80s, The Knights of Labor (KOL) wage worker's union is estimated to have recruited between 60-80,000 African American workers into its membership.

The American Federation of Labor, a craft union, also began to recruit some craft and skilled African American workers into its ranks, but in far less numbers than KOL. Yet, the vast majority of African American workers were still not represented by any union and had to fend for themselves for fair wages and decent working conditions.

Finally, in 1925, African Americans organized the Brotherhood of Sleeping Car Porters union under the leadership of Asa Philip Randolph. It was the first nation-wide African American union. Since thousands were employed in the Pullman railroad industry as porters, car cleaners, cooks, waiters and stokers, this action brought about not only better working conditions and salary but also helped to bring about a greater sense of solidarity among these workers themselves.

It wasn't until shortly before World War II and some years afterwards, that larger numbers of African Americans were recruited and integrated into another national union, the Congress of Industrial Organizations (CIO), led by John L. Lewis.

8. The U.S. Supreme Court decision of 1954 not only struck down racial segregation and discrimination at all levels of public school education, but it also had an effect on other major institutions in American society. For example, many predominantly white Christian religious organizations started to desegregate and take affirmative action to open their membership and leadership to African Americans and other minorities.

9. Former President Jimmy Carter and his wife, Rosalyn, threatened to withdraw their membership in their hometown Baptist church in Plains, Georgia, unless the church did away with its racial discriminaton policies.

    Their church eventually did so, and in time so did the entire Southern Baptist Convention with whom the local Plains church was affiliated.

    Also, early in his naval cadet years at the U.S. Naval Academy, Jimmy Carter had spoken out against the racism expressed there by some white cadets against Westly Brown, an African American cadet whom Carter had befriended.

10. Professional sports such as baseball, football, and basketball did not freely begin recruiting and employing African American athletes until after World War II. Baseball trailblazers in 1947 were Jackie Robinson for the Brooklyn Dodgers and Larry Doby for the Cleveland Indians; Marion Motley, football player for the Cleveland Browns in 1948; and Chuck Cooper, basketball player for the Boston Celtics in 1951.

EBONY OWL: DID YOU KNOW?

Institutional slavery and racism in America must be understood as very complex and deeply entrenched systems of behavior that involved many of the nation's most basic institutions for more than 300 years.

These systems of human oppression were forced on African and African American people against their will, and at the time were rationalized and morally justified by white racist ideology and theology. Then they were enforced by laws and legal systems by those having the power to do so at various levels of government.

Also, such extra-legal terrorist groups like the Ku Klux Klan and the White Knights of Camelia used threats and violence to re-

inforce white racism.

The legacy of white racism in America has had devastating and horrendous consequences for many African American individuals, families, institutions, and community life as well as for some other Americans.

For many generations up to the present, it has denied thousands the opportunity to self-actualize, develop their potential abilities, and ultimately make their contribution to American society.

Although it is not as openly blatant as it was in the past, racism still persists in the U.S. today at both the covert and overt levels of behavior.

Fortunately, there are now laws and a growing sentiment among most Americans to eradicate this "ism" and others like it.

It remains to be seen in the 21st century whether the nation as a whole will formally take steps to acknowledge this devastating, hypocritical, and immoral part of its history and take effective steps to resolve the problem and make fair and just restitution.

1. In 1833, a nationwide "American Anti-Slavery Society" was established by an interracial group of Americans. Its purpose was to advocate and take action to abolish slavery in the U.S.

    Some of the prominent white Americans in the organization were persons like activist and publisher William L. Garrison, wealthy New Yorker Arthur Tappan, and well-known African Americans including Samuel Cornish, Robert Purvis, and eventually Frederick Douglass, among others.

    However, prior to this formal organization, there were free African Americans like Prince Hall, Richard Allen, Sojourner Truth, and David Walker, who were already speaking out against slavery and assisting abolition efforts.

2. In 1790, when Benjamin Franklin was president of the Quaker Abolitionist Society in Philadelphia, Pennsylvania, the organization made a formal petition to the U.S. Congress to abolish slavery.

   It was rejected, and in response to political pressure from southern slave owners, Congress simply continued to debate the issue of slavery and did nothing to curtail its growth and development, and its impact on the whole nation.

3. Frederick Douglass. In 1847, after moving to Rochester, New York, he started publishing an abolitionist paper called, "The North Star."

   Martin Delaney, who published one of the first African American newspapers in Pittsburgh, Pennsylvania, went to New York to help Douglass edit "The North Star." Later, Delaney studied medicine at Harvard and became a medical doctor.

4. In 1829, David Walker, who was living in Boston, published one of the first and most militant pamphlets ever written against slavery.

   It was commonly known as the "Appeal," and it strongly urged African people all over the world to violently rebel against slavery and white domination.

   Its message was thought to be extremely threatening to the interests of the pro-slavery states, and also considered so highly inflammatory in tone, that was officially banned in many Southern states.

5. Rev. Henry Highland Garnet, a highly educated minister of the only African American Presbyterian Church in New York. His speech entitled, "Call to Rebellion," was similar in tone to David Walker's "Appeal" because it urged African Americans to resist slavery by any means necessary, including armed rebellion.

   Later in his life, Garnet was a delegate to the World Peace Congress in Europe, and in 1865, was one of the first African American ministers to give a religious speech to the U.S. House of Representatives.

6. Sojourner Truth. At age 30, when she was still known by her slave name, "Isabella" or "Belle," she was able to get her freedom with the help of some Quakers. In 1843, after having a mystical religious experience in which she believed that God was calling her, she began to travel and speak out against slavery, and then took the name, "Sojourner Truth."

Afterwards, her plain-talk speeches and personal charisma resulted in her being invited to give antislavery speeches in different parts of the northeast. She would also speak out for women's rights. During the Civil War she also helped to nurse wounded soldiers and to get supplies for them and other persons in need, particularly in the Washington, D.C. area.

7. In 1800, Gabriel Prosser, a twenty-five-year-old slave, planned and led some 1,000 other slaves to march toward Richmond, Virginia for the purpose of getting control of the city and especially its federal arsenal of guns and munitions.

   In 1821, Denmark Vesey, a 54-year-old middle-age African American former slave, who had bought his freedom after winning a lottery, secretly organized a plan that would involve nearly 9,000 slaves and former slaves. At a designated time they were to revolt and militarily take control of Charleston, South Carolina.

   However, in the case of both of these planned revolts, there were informant slaves who told the authorities. Consequently, both men were arrested, convicted, and hanged as leaders of the potential revolts.

8. In 1831, Nat Turner, considered by his peers to be a highly intelligent and religious mystic, organized an estimated 60 to 80 slaves in a militant and violent uprising against white slave holders in Southampton, Virginia.

   He and his followers killed 57 whites, old and young. It was the most deadly slave revolt in U.S. history and resulted in a very punitive backlash against African Americans generally, and specifically toward any antislavery advocates.

   After Turner's execution, enraged whites indiscriminately killed more than 200 slaves in Southampton.

9. John Brown. This 60-year-old, tall and thin looking white-haired man, with a group of twenty-two men, five of them African American, attacked and took control of the U.S. federal arsenal and munitions depot at Harper's Ferry, Virginia, in 1859.

   Following their successful attack, a contingent of Marines successfully stormed the building which Brown and his men held, killed two of them during the siege, and arrested and eventually hanged the rest, including John Brown.

   Brown soon became a martyr for many African Americans and many others who were against slavery. The American folk song, "Old John Brown's Body Lies a Moldering in the Grave," and different versions of it, became a very popular song for some Union soldiers during the Civil war, and remains a popular American folk song even today.

10. Oberlin University and Western Reserve University in Ohio.

Although the Quaker religious group voiced a strong protest against slavery as early as the 17th century, it wasn't until the 1800s that a proactive and militant anti-slavery movement began to publicly emerge and gain momentum. One of the most militant examples of this was John Brown's attack on Harper's Ferry.

Regarding the action of John Brown against slavery, Frederick Douglass wrote the following:

"Posterity will owe everlasting thanks to John Brown. He has attacked slavery with the weapons precisely adapted to bring it to death. Moral considerations have long been exhausted upon slaveholders. It is vain to reason with them.... Slavery is a system of brute force. It shields itself behind might, rather than right. It must be met with its own weapons."

1. At the beginning of the Civil War both Frederick Douglass and Sojourner Truth met with President Lincoln in an attempt to convince him to recruit free African Americans and fugitive slaves to serve in the Union Army. However, it wasn't until May 1863 that Lincoln gave his permission as commander-in-chief to allow the War Department to officially recruit and enlist African Americans in the Union Army.

2. An estimated 186,000 served in the Union Army and were officially designated as the "United States Colored Troops" (USCT). They were organized into five segregated regiments: infantry, cavalry, engineers, and light and heavy artillery units.

   Nearly 30,000 served in the Union Navy, and another 50,000 men and women served as nurses and attendants for the sick and wounded.

   The total number of casualties for the USCT was 38,000; for the Union Army was 364,511, and for the Confederates was 133,821.

3. The 54th Regiment of Massachusetts Volunteers of African Descent. They were under the command of Colonel Robert G. Shaw, a young, white 29-year-old Harvard graduate, who lost his life along with many of his soldiers in a battle against the Confederate Army at Fort Wagner, South Carolina.

The African American Quiz Book

4. In 1862, a slave who became known as Robert Smalls disguised himself as an assistant to the ship's captain, and with a crew of other slaves and his family cleverly captured a Confederate steamboat, the *Planter,* and sailed it out of the harbor at Charleston, South Carolina.

   Afterwards, they turned it over to the Union Navy, and Smalls was given a reward for the capture. After the war, Smalls was first elected to the South Carolina State Legislature and then to the U.S. Congress. (His great-grandson, Robert Smalls III, lives in New York City.)

5. One battle was when the USCT 7th Regiment, under the command of General Ulysses Grant, captured the Confederate Fort Gilmer, located near Richmond, Virginia, in the fall of 1864.

   A second crucial battle was the defeat of the Confederates at Fort Fisher in Wilmington, North Carolina, by the USCT 1st Regiment in January of 1865.

6. The USCT took part in some 450 military engagements, including 39 major battles, mostly in the last two years of the war.

   During this time, sixteen USCT soldiers were awarded Congressional Medals of Honor. Sergeant William H. Carney of the heroic 54th Massachusetts and James Harris of the 38th USCT were two of first African American soldiers to receive the award.

7. More than 7,000 were commissioned officers who served as chaplains and doctors, mainly for USCT. White officers were assigned to all command positions over USCT. There were no African American naval officers, and none until nearly 100 years later.

8. a. Mary E. Bowser was a freed slave who gathered intelligence information about the Confederate forces when they were headquartered in Richmond, Virginia. She was sometimes called "Crazy Bet," because she would pretend childlike behavior. In fact, she was clever enough to gather reliable information from slaves and others close to Jefferson Davis and his Confederate Army, and then pass it on to Union General Grant.

   b. Elizabeth H. Keckley was dressmaker for two president's wives during the Civil War. Ironically, she first worked for Varina Howell Davis, wife of Confederate President Jefferson Davis, and then for Mary Todd Lincoln, President Abraham Lincoln's wife. There are indications that Keckley became a trusted friend of Mary Lincoln as well as her dressmaker, and may have had a direct influence on Mrs. Lincoln and an indirect one on the President, especially as a liaison with African American leaders.

After the Civil War, Keckley is given credit for organizing and administering a charitable relief agency for the freed slaves.

c. As a young slave in Savannah, Georgia, Susie King Baker secretly learned how to read and write even though it was against the law. When the Union Army defeated the Confederate forces in her area, she started classes to teach both slave children and some adults how to read and write. She also volunteered as a nurse caring for sick and wounded soldiers. Her role model for helping and serving others, as it was for many other women at the time, was Clara Barton, founder of the American Red Cross. It is now known that countless numbers of African American women traveled with USCT regiments as nurses, laundresses, cooks, and sometimes in a military capacity.

9. As a result of her knowledge and experience of traveling back and forth to the South assisting runaway slaves, Harriet Tubman became a very cunning and shrewd spy. She was also a scout for the Union Army. She not only gathered intelligence information about the Confederate forces, but provided food and nursing care for some of the USCT.

10. In 1972 a memorial statute was placed in Baltimore, Maryland's, "Battle Monument Plaza," to honor African Americans who had served in the Civil War and all U.S. wars, including the Vietnam War.

EBONY QUIZ: DID YOU KNOW?

Once President Lincoln reluctantly allowed both free and slave African Americans to fight on the Union side, the military successes of the Confederates began to decline.

African American soldiers and sailors fought with valor and distinction. They were motivated and determined not only to defeat the Confederates, but to free themselves and the nation from the devastating effects of slavery.

After the war, African Americans continued their struggle.

In the preface of the 1965 edition of his book, "The Negro's Civil War," James M. McPherson writes the following:

"The Negro was not merely a passive recipient of the benefits conferred upon him by the war. Negro orators and writers provided leadership in the struggle for emancipation and equal rights. Blacks were active in the movements to bring education, suffrage, and land to Southern freedmen. And perhaps most important of all,

the contribution of Negro soldiers helped the North win the war and convinced many Northern people the Negro deserved to be treated as a man and equal."

1. After the end of the Civil War in 1865, thousands of soldiers who were veterans of the U.S. Colored Troops were reorganized into new infantry, artillery and cavalry regiments in 1866. The 9th and 10th Cavalries, and the 24th and 25th Infantry regiments, were their official designations.

   As they came into contact with Native American Indian (NIA) tribes, especially the Cheyenne, they were often referred to as "Buffalo Soldiers" because of their hair texture, their use of buffalo skins for blankets, and their toughness in battle.

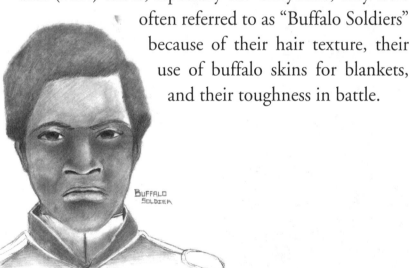

BUFFALO SOLDIER

2. The primary task of the Buffalo Soldiers was to protect the white settlers who were migrating to new lands west of the Mississippi River that were now available for homesteading.

   The responsibility given to the Buffalo Soldiers was described as the "pacification" of the new frontier, and to protect the migration and settlement from hostile Native American Indians and outlaws, as well as to prevent lawlessness among the settlers.

   Historians often refer to this period of mass migration in the 19th century as the "Westward Movement."

3. Most of the 9th and 10th Cavalry troopers were former enlistees in the Union Army who came from both slave and free-person backgrounds. Life in the military provided them with more economic and occupational stability and benefits than they could get in civilian life.

4. All of the commanders of the Buffalo Soldiers (Col. Edward Hatch, Maj. Albert Morrow and Lt. Col. Wesley Merritt) were veteran white career Union Army Cavalry officers. At first they were reluctant to command USCT soldiers because of the persistent and erroneous stereotype that they did not make good soldiers. But contrary to their initial expectations, the 9th Cavalry trained to be one of the most disciplined and tough fighting regiments.

The 10th Cavalry Buffalo Soldiers were under the command of Col. Benjamin Grierson, who was basically trained in music. However, during the Civil War, he was recognized by Gen. Ulysses Grant as a daring and courageous Cavalry officer, and under his leadership the Buffalo Soldiers won a number of important battles against the Apache, Comanche, and Sioux Indian tribes.

5. The war with the Cheyennes in 1867-69, and the war with the Apaches in 1875-1876 that led to the capture of their chief, Geronimo.

Hundreds of Buffalo Soldiers served with the 9th and 10th Cavalries and fought in some 100 battles against various Indian tribes. Eighteen received Congressional Medals of Honor for their bravery.

6. They surveyed, mapped, and built hundreds of miles of new roads, located water and other natural resources, protected wagon trains and stagecoaches, and helped to maintain law and order for the homesteaders settling in new parts of the West.

7. Generally, the settlers were appreciative, looked favorably on their duties, and felt secure with the military presence of the Buffalo Soldiers, except for those who were pro-Confederate and racist in their attitude. The Native Americans thought of them as "good warriors."

8. Theodore "Teddy" Roosevelt. Before becoming president, he fought with the 9th and 10th Cavalry units as a Colonel with the Rough Riders during the battle and siege of San Juan Hill, Cuba, in the 1898 Spanish-American War.

   He commended the Buffalo Soldiers for their courage and bravery on the battlefield right after the war, but he also made some disparaging comments about them.

   During the same war, Buffalo Soldiers with the 24th and 25th Infantry regiments left San Francisco and went to the Philippine Islands. Their mission was to put down Filipino resistance to the new U.S. military control over their country following the defeat of the Spanish during the Spanish-American War.

9. General John J. Pershing who commanded the 10th Calvary in his military attacks against Pancho Villa and his army in Mexico in 1916.

   Pershing also had African American troops under his command during World War I, and as a result was tagged with the nickname, "Black Jack." This did not mean that he had a completely unbiased and positive attitude toward the soldiering of African American troops. For example, while commanding them in France, he would not allow French military authorities to treat them on an integrated non-discriminatory basis as the French wished to do.

10. In 1992, a life-size bronze monument was dedicated to honor the patriotism and heroism of the Buffalo Soldiers on a site at Fort Leavenworth, Kansas. Four-star General Colin Powell, Senator Bob Dole, and Kansas Governor Joan Finney, as well as others, took part in the ceremony.

Although the Buffalo Soldiers served with distinction on the American western frontier, there is no doubt that they had mixed feelings about fighting and pacifying the Plains Indians. This is because they were well aware of the fact that the Cherokee, Creek, and Seminole had given refuge to former runaway slaves, and that after the Civil War they also accepted many of the runaways into their tribal communities.

It was also known that some African Americans had married into these tribes as well as into others. This eventually gave rise to the term "Black Indians."

They were also aware that some of their military assignments were primarilly to protect the economic interests of the Union Pacific Railroad and the Central Pacific Railroad rather than the safety and security of the settlers.

Although the transcontinental railroad linked New York with San Francisco, some of the tracks were laid on lands misappropriated from Native American Indian tribes by treaties and stealth.

1. Nat Love was born in Tennessee in 1854, and as a young man worked as a cowpuncher on his travels to Dodge City, Kansas, and as far northwest as Deadwood, Montana. It was here that he earned his nickname, "Deadwood Dick," because of his exceptional horseriding skills and marksmanship with a rifle.

2. Bill Pickett, who at rodeo shows would dismount from his galloping horse, wrestle a steer by its horns to a stop, then twist the steer's head upward while biting and holding on to the steer's upper lip like a bulldog. He would then throw the steer down to the ground and quickly tie its feet to complete the act.

   This "bulldogging" technique he devised made him famous and resulted in his taking part in rodeos throughout the U.S., England, and South America. He also traveled with the legendary cowboy actor Tom Mix and humorist Will Rogers.

   In 1971, Pickett was elected to the National Cowboy Hall of Fame in Oklahoma City, where there is a large photo exhibit and other information about him.

3. George Fletcher developed quite a name for himself in Oregon and across the nation as a tough cowpuncher who could tame the wildest bucking horse.

   In 1911, he was the first African American to win the National Cowboy Bucking Contest. He won again in 1921. In 1969, he was elected to the Pendleton Roundup Hall of Fame in Oregon.

4. a. Young Cranford Goldsby earned the infamous nickname "Cherokee Bill" as one of the fastest gunmen and outlaws in the Oklahoma Indian Territory in the 1890s. He worked as a scout with the Cherokee, Creek, and Seminole Indian tribes before turning to outlaw gang life.

Eventually, he was arrested as a dangerous outlaw, and Hanging Judge Parker sentenced him to be hung at Fort Smith, Arkansas. A large crowd watched the hanging.

b. Wearing his large sombrero hat and carrying his sidearm and rifle, Ben Hodges presented himself as a "bad hombre" in his Dodge City, Kansas, hangouts.

He also claimed to be a legitimate benefactor of former Spanish land grants in Texas and under false pretenses sold plots of land. As a result, he swindled gullible investors out of considerable amounts of money in various land-for-sale schemes.

5. Willie Kennard was a former Buffalo Soldier who accepted the challenging and dangerous job as U.S. marshal in Yankee Hill. His formidable bravery helped to gradually bring law and order to this Colorado town.

6. Both William Robinson and George Monroe were pioneer Pony Express riders in California. Robinson rode in the Stockton and nearby gold mining areas.

George Monroe gained national recognition as a trusted stagecoach rider because of driving President Ulysses S. Grant into the Yosemite Valley in 1879. Today, a citation in the historic and popular Yosemite Wawona Hotel recognizes his achievements. And, on a roadside in Yosemite Park, there is a sign designating a "Monroe Meadow" area.

7. Mary Fields. Although born a slave in Tennessee in 1832, Mary Fields ran away to Ohio, and was eventually hired to assist a group of Catholic nuns in the 1880s. She went with them to Cascade, Montana, to help them start a Catholic mission for Native Americans.

During this time she drove a stagecoach to carry supplies and freight for the nuns and others. Because of her reputed ability to physically box, use a gun, and be as tough as any man, she was highly respected in the community, especially as the person who protected as well as helped the nuns.

For eight years she carried U.S. Government mail, and in doing so earned the nickname "Stagecoach Mary." At her funeral, the citizens of Cascade spoke very highly of all of the good things she had done in her town.

8. Jim Beckwourth, the son of a Virginia slave, became an adopted member of the Crow Indian tribe. He was a fur trapper and developed a reputation as a rugged mountain man.

    In Northern California near the headwaters of the Feather River, there is a much-traveled mountain pass through the Sierra Nevada mountains at an elevation of 5,221 ft. that Beckwourth discovered, and it soon became more easily traversed than the Donner Pass.

    Today, the pass is officially named Beckwourth Pass to commemorate his discovery. The pass accommodates U.S. highway 70, and the Western Pacific Railroad line. The small town of Beckwourth is nearby.

9. George Washington Bush was a well-to-do free African American cattle ranger who sought land and freedom in the Oregon Territory. Prior to his arrival, and unknown to Bush, the Oregon provincial government had taken action to forbid the settlement of "Negroes" in the territory. This forced Bush and others to settle farther north on land parcels that eventually became a part of the state of Washington.

10. Approximately 8,000 in the western U.S.. Today there are some 20,000 registered with the National Black Cowboys Association.

Several decades before and after the Civil War, hundreds of African Americans, free and slave, were a part of the U.S. Westward Movement. Those who were free had been lured by dreams to settle in California and Oregon where they thought they would be free from racial segregation and discrimination and to have a better life.

However, little did they realize that they would have to compete with thousands of European immigrants who had also been lured to the West to prospect for gold and to have their own farmland.

Thus, African Americans usually had to work at the most physically demanding and financially least-rewarding jobs. The men found work as horse handlers, bronco busters, low-level cowhands and cooks. The women found work as laundry workers, domestics and also as cooks.

QUIZ 14 ANSWERS

The Origin of Early African American Churches and Pioneer Religious Leaders

1. Most African slaves came from different tribal religions that were spiritually and ritualistically oriented. Some believed in one supreme god (monotheism) while others focused on many gods (polytheism).

   Other slaves were Muslims who came from various parts of West Africa that had come under the influence of Arabian Muslims beginning in the 8th century.

   Kunta Kinte, a captured slave depicted in Alex Haley's saga, "Roots," was of Muslim religious background.

   Beginning with the initial arrival of African slaves, different Protestant religious communities gradually began to proselytize them in order to make them converts to their particular Christian beliefs and practices. This was usually done in a very ethnocentric and racially patronizing manner.

   As a result of being segregated in worship services and not being fully accepted as members and leaders in these early white Christian churches, African American Christians began to develop their own separate churches.

Today, these early churches represent a synthesis of African religious traditions and mostly various evangelical Protestant denominational models.

Equally important, a diversity of very meaningful styles of worship, organizational structures, programs and activities, and leadership arrangements unique to these churches began to develop and still exist today.

Currently, the five largest African American church denominations in terms of membership are: National Baptist Convention U.S.A., Inc.(5,000,000), National Baptist Missionary Convention (2,500,000), Progressive National Baptist Convention, Inc. (2,500,000), The African Methodist Episcopal Church (2,311,400), and The Church of God in Christ (5,000,000).

2. In 1793, Richard Allen, a former slave in Delaware, joined with Absalom Jones and others to organize the Bethel Church in Philadelphia, Pennsylvania. It later became the center for formally organizing the African Methodist Episcopal Church that still exists today. They felt compelled to organize their own church because the white Methodist church they were attending segregated them and would not allow them to participate freely.

3. One of the earliest organized African American Baptist congregations was in Silver Bluff, North Carolina, in 1773, with David George as its prominent preacher.

   In 1788, the first African Baptist Church was founded in Savannah, Georgia. Both Andrew Byron and George Liele were outstanding preachers at this time.

   Over the years African American Baptists have organized themselves into three major conventions as cited above in answer number 1. They have a combined total membership of more than 10 million, and all three conventions are predominantly African American in membership and leadership.

4. In 1801, James Varick, a former slave, became one of the founders and first bishops of the African Methodist Episcopal Zion churches in New York. Later in 1827, Varick, John Russwurm, Richard Allen, Alexander Crumwell, and others started the first widely read African American newspaper in the U.S.: "Freedom's Journal."

5. Lemuel Haynes was a racially-mixed child born in Connecticut who eventually lived and worked as a house servant for a family in Massachusetts. He volunteered and distinguished himself as a minuteman in the Massachusetts militia during the Revolutionary War, fighting in the place of his owner's son.

   After the war he received his freedom, and through his own efforts learned how to read, especially the Bible.

   Eventually, he became an excellent preacher, was ordained, and then was called to pastor a number of all-white Congregational churches in New England.

6. In 1821, Lott Cary, a former slave, was commissioned by the African Baptist Missionary Society of Richmond, Virginia, to do missionary work in the newly created U.S. African American colony of Liberia.

   Daniel Coker, also a former slave, went as an African Methodist Episcopal missionary to Sierra Leone, Africa, about a year earlier than Carey. His support came mainly from the American Colonization Society.

   Both men served out their years in Africa and through their pioneering efforts accomplished a great deal in establishing missionary programs and the foundation for their respective church denominations in Africa.

7. In 1854, James Augustine Healy was one of the first African Americans to be ordained as a Roman Catholic priest.

He received his theological education and training at Canadian and French seminaries, was appointed pastor of the Cathedral of the Holy Cross and St. James Cathedral in Boston, and then appointed bishop over Catholic parishes in Maine and New Hampshire in 1875.

In 1874, his younger brother, Patrick Francis Healy, a highly educated Jesuit priest, became the first African American to be appointed President of Georgetown University in Washington, D.C.

Both men were of racially- and ethnically-mixed family background with eight other siblings. Their father was Irish and owned a large plantation in Georgia. His wife, Mary, was a racially-mixed African American woman, and both had a deep love for each other and their children.

8. In 1829, this first Catholic order of African American nuns was created in Baltimore, Maryland, to help provide an orphanage and education for abandoned African American youth.

The order became known as the Oblate Sisters of Providence and was highly praised for its unselfish service.

9. a. Henry McNeal Turner was a free man and in 1863 became the first African American minister to be appointed by President Lincoln to serve as a chaplain in the Union Army.

After the war, he was elected to the Georgia state legislature where he served for several years until forced out of office by its racist politics.

b. Allen Allensworth, a former escaped slave from Kentucky, served in the Union Army during the Civil War. After returning to civilian life and undertaking formal studies, he became a minister.

Afterwards, he returned to the army, was commissioned, and served as a chaplain for the all African American 24th Infantry for nearly 20 years. He retired with a rank of Lt. Colonel.

In 1908, he led a group of African Americans to settle in central California near Fresno. After incorporation it became the state's first all African American town, Allensworth. Today, the former town has been restored and has been fully developed into the Colonel Allensworth State Historic Park, located not far from Fresno.

10. In 1804, Absalom Jones was ordained as a priest in the Episcopal Church, and in 1989, Barbara C. Harris was the first woman and African American to become a bishop in the Episcopal Church.

EBONY OWL: DID YOU KNOW?

Most African Americans are Protestant Christians and are members of mostly Baptist denominational churches. Theologically they may be thought of as essentially evangelical Christians in spite of their denominational diversity.

Also, collectively, African Americans are one of the largest evangelical religious populations in the U.S. because of their emphasis on the following basic beliefs:

• God is in control of human history as revealed in Jesus Christ.

• The Bible is the basic authority for one's religious faith.

• Spiritual conversion and baptism are

prerequisites to Christian living.
• Marriage and family are sacred God-given institutions.
• Individual Christians and their churches must be "doers of the word and not hearers only!"
• Equal opportunity and social justice.
• Emphasis on morality in individual relations, work, business, the media, entertainment industry, and in government.
Only a small number of African Americans are Buddhists, Jews, Muslims or members of other religious groups.

Please note:
All church membership figures above are taken from the 2003 Yearbook of American and Canadian Churches.

QUIZ 15 ANSWERS

Little Known African American Inventors, Engineers, Medical Doctors and Scientists

1. Norbert Rillieux received a U.S. patent (No. 4879) for a new sugar-refining machine in 1843. His machine not only sped up the process to refine sugar cane into granules, but it also produced a superior quality product that could be readily used commercially, as well as in the home.

2. In 1901, Granville T. Woods received a U.S. patent (No. 667,110) for a third-rail switching system design for use on electric railways. Today, many of the third-rail electrical systems used on mass transportation systems throughout the world are based on his basic invention. He was also granted patents for other prototype inventions related to the telephone and telegraph communication systems.

3. Lewis Latimer and Joseph V. Nichols, a white American with whom he worked, received a U.S. patent (No. 247,097) in 1881 for their invention of an electric lamp.

It was made of a pear-shaped glass housing with a wire carbon filament inside, and although Thomas A. Edison had invented the incandescent light bulb in 1879, Latimer and Nichols' carbon filament was a tremendous improvement over Edison's.

Their light bulb filament produced a brighter and longer lasting glow of light when electric current was transmitted through the bulb.

4. In 1923, Garrett A. Morgan received a U.S. patent (No. 1,475,024) for an automatic traffic signal light system for the purpose of regulating vehicle and pedestrian traffic at intersections.

Nine years earlier in 1914, he was issued a U.S. patent (No. 1,113,675) for a "Breathing Device," or gas mask. He successfully used the mask himself along with others to rescue workers in the Erie Canal 1916 tunnel disaster. He was widely commended for his rescue efforts.

In the 21st century, modifications of these inventions are used daily in many parts of the world.

5. In the summer of 1893, Dr. Daniel Hale Williams, faced with an emergency situation at Provident Hospital in Chicago, performed what is now considered to be one of the first successful open heart surgeries in the U.S.

   This outstanding achievement resulted in his becoming a member of the all-white American College of Surgeons. He was also honored for his efforts that greatly improved the medical services at Provident Hospital, and later on at the Freedmen's Hospital in Washington, D.C.

6. Charles Drew's leadership qualities were recognized early during his days at Amherst College in Massachusetts, where he received honors both as an athlete and student.

   Following his graduation from Amherst in 1933, Drew completed his medical studies at McGill University in Montreal, Canada, where he earned degrees as Master of Surgery and Doctor of Medicine.

   After years of research focusing on blood composition, he successfully developed procedures for storing blood plasma. During World War II, his method became the standard for blood plasma transfusions in England in 1940, for the American Red Cross, and eventually for the U.S. Armed Forces.

7. George Washington Carver was born in 1860 to slave parents on a plantation in Missouri. Since he was prevented from getting a high school education in Kansas because of his race, it wasn't until 1891, at age 25, that he was able to begin college.

First he attended Simpson College in Iowa for two years; he then went to Iowa State University (ISU) in Ames, where he earned his masters degree in 1896.

After graduating from ISU, Booker T. Washington, Principal of Tuskegee Institute in Alabama, invited him to teach at Tuskegee and organize an agricultural education program.

After a life's work of some fifty years at Tuskegee, where his genius as a botanist and agricultural researcher flourished, he was given both national and worldwide recognition for his many achievements as an outstanding agricultural scientist.

Peanut butter is only one of the food products he developed, something that is enjoyed by many the world over.

8. John Stanard received a patent (No. 455,891) for a refrigerator that became known popularly as an "ice-box" because of its primary use to store ice inside of a chest or cabinet in order to keep the contents that were put inside cold.

   Some 50 years later in 1949, Frederick M. Jones, an African American orphan with only a formal sixth-grade education, invented a refrigeration system for trucks in 1949 (Patent No. 2,475,841) and for refrigerating boxcars (Patent No. 2,780,923).

9. In 1896, Charles B. Brooks patented a design for a street sweeper (No. 556,711) that became a prototype for many types of street sweepers that are used throughout the U.S. today.

10. At the turn of the century when the game of golf was gaining popularity in the U.S., George F. Grant, a golfer, hit on the idea of inventing a golf tee.

    He thought that a small wooden peg-shaped stand on which the golf ball could rest would make it a lot easier to hit the ball, rather than hitting it from the ground or a small mound of dirt.

    His simple and useful invention quickly caught on, and interestingly, he was not the typical inventor, but a dentist.

EBONY OWL: DID YOU KNOW?

From the late 1700s to the present 21st century, many talented African American inventors, medical professionals, educators, scientists and researchers have and are making significant contributions to the technological progress and improved quality of life for all Americans, as well as for people around the world.

A current example of a talented medical professional is Dr. Ben Carson, director of neurosurgery at John Hopkins Children's Center in Baltimore, MD. He has performed a number of very delicate successful brain surgeries for persons in the U.S. and from abroad. He is considered one of the world's most expert brain surgeons.

Dr. Mae Jemison, first African American woman astronaut in NASA, is another exceptionally talented individual. She is not only a chemical engineer, but has also worked as a doctor improving people's health care in Cambodia and Africa. She is also founder of the Jemison Group, Inc., operating to assist various charitable causes.

Omissions are great crimes of history
by Randall Robinson
Oakland Tribune—June 26, 2005

I can still see the "Boston Globe" front-page picture of the broadly grinning South African surgeon Christiaan Barnard, a privileged product of the world's ugliest race-based dictatorship, who had just become "the first person to successfully transplant a human heart." Performed at Cape Town's Groote Schuur Hospital, this made Barnard an international celebrity and conferred upon white-supremacist government a measure of legitimacy.

On May 29, 2005, Hamilton Naki, a black South African, died in penniless obscurity at 78. It was he who, with extraordinary and painstaking skill, removed the heart of Denise Darvall, a white woman who had been in an automobile accident, and presented it to Barnard for the second part of the procedure, its placement in Louis Washkansky, a 55 year old diabetic. Detrmined to rewrite history, Groote Schuur Hospital admonished Naki, "Nobody must know what you are doing."

Those who spotted Naki on the periphery of photos recording the historic moment were told that he was a "cleaner and gardener." This is how Groote Schuur Hospital's records — for 50 years — described the man who led the first of two surgical procedures that produced the first successful heart transplant.

Growing up in Ngcingane, a small village in the Eastern Cape, Naki went without shoes and wrapped himself in sheepskin to ward off the winter cold. He was lashed as a "kaffir" (a subhuman) by whites, routinely arrested under various apartheid regulations and subjected to endless humiliation.

After he was forced to leave school at 14, one of his early jobs involved holdiing animals while doctors operated on them. "I stole with my eyes," he once said, explaining how he eventually became extraordinarily adept at organ transplants in general and liver transplants in particular. Groote Schuur Hospital had him secretly teach medical students professors and perform surgery right up until his retirement in 1991. For the entirety of his working life, he had no running water, no electricity, and no reliable transportation. To the world, even to his neighbors in ramshackle Langa township near Cape Town, "(the state) pretended like I was a cleaner." In retirement, Naki received a gardener's pension of $127 a month.

Without Naki, Barnard's historic heart transplant might never have happened. Said Barnard, "On Saturday, I was a surgeon in South Africa, very little known. On Monday, I was world-renowned." Just before Barnard died a few years ago, he confessed that Naki "probably had more technical skill than I had."

What we choose to remember and to forget, what we choose to include and to exclude, has enormous consequence for all who look to history for a measure of their worth.

The abuse of history-telling discretion has had life-and-death significance for our relations with more than a few of the world's peoples — the Vietnamese, the Somalis, the Haitians, the Iraqis.

No one outside South Africa had heard of Hamilton Naki before his death. It is also a good bet that neither Barnard nor Naki nor 1 in 1 million Americans knows that African doctors routinely performed cataract surgery at Sankore University in Timbuktu, Mali, in the 13th century.

For 246 years, slavery throughout the Americas snuffed out the lives of millions and robbed victims of their material worth. Even more damaging, and with asphyxiating patience, it erased from us all memory of the documentable glories of Africa's golden antiquity.

In studious denial, our country today lives with the cost and shame of this, its own holocaust. Our prisons warehouse the evidence. People seldom over-perform or under-perform the record of performance relentlessly presented to them as the full measure of their value.

For all concerned, the cost of ignorance is enormous. Just consider the gulled American farm-boy soldier fighting in Iraq who has never heard of Gertrude Bell or Percy Cox or the mistold exploits of Col. Thomas Edward Lawrence, the so-called Lawrence of Arabia.

QUIZ 16 ANSWERS
Trailblazers and Visionary Leaders in American Education

1. In 1823, Alexander Twilight graduated from Middlebury College in Vermont, and is considered to be the first African American to earn a college degree in the U.S..

    Coincidentally, Dr. Howard Dean, a Democratic Party candidate for U.S. President in 2004, is also a graduate of Middlebury College.

2. Mary Jane Patterson graduated with a B.A. from Oberlin College in Ohio in 1862. Her parents were fugitive slaves who were able to escape from Raleigh, North Carolina, and eventually settle in Ohio, a non-slave state.

    In Oberlin, Ohio African Americans had the freedom and opportunity to pursue an education, so Mary Jane was able to attend and graduate from Oberlin College.

    She spent most of her life as a dedicated pioneer teacher and principal at schools for African American students in both Philadelphia and Washington D.C.

3. Book Talioferro Washington was born in 1856 on a slave plantation in Virginia. After his parents migrated to West Virginia, he had to work at various jobs to supplement his family's income.

Eager to get an education, at the age of sixteen he walked many miles from his home in Malden, West Virginia, to attend Hampton Normal and Agricultural School in Hampton, Virginia.

While a student at Hampton, Washington's exceptional academic achievements, his desire to educate others, and his apparent leadership potential greatly impressed Samuel Armstrong, founder of the institute and Union Army officer.

After Washington's graduation he worked as a teacher at Hampton, and Armstrong, recognizing his ability, recommended that he organize a similar school for a group of citizens in Tuskegee, Alabama.

Washington accepted their offer, and with very meager funds he started Tuskegee Normal and Industrial Institute in 1881, which has evolved into Tuskegee University.

Today, Tuskegee is recognized as one of Alabama's highly accredited institutions, offering more than 50 majors through its five colleges: College of Agricultural, Environmental, and Natural Sciences; College of Business and Information Science; College of Engineering, Architecture, and Physical Sciences; College of Liberal Arts and Education; and College of Veterinary Medicine, Nursing and Allied Health.

4. In 1867, Howard Normal and Theological Institute for the Education of Teachers and Preachers was founded as a part of Congress' Reconstruction efforts to educate freed slaves and others.

   The school was under the authority of the Freedman's Bureau and the leadership of former Union Army General Oliver Howard, after whom the school was named.

   With support from the First Congregational Society of Washington, D.C., a curriculum was developed and financial help given, as well as money provided by Congress.

   Initially, African American youth were enrolled as well as some white students, and in a short time, the Institute was designated as Howard University and began to receive some of its funding directly from Congress.

   Howard University's first African American president, Dr. Mordecai W. Johnson, was appointed in 1926. Under his 34-year administration the university's overall undergraduate and graduate programs and curriculum, as well as physical facilities, greatly improved and expanded.

At the beginning of the 21st century Howard University is one of the finest academic institutions of higher learning in the U.S., offering more than 80 undergraduate majors, and graduate and professional studies in 61 areas, that include 27 doctoral degrees.

Its distinguished faculty and alumni of the past and present have made significant achievements in various career fields in the U.S. and many places abroad.

5. In 1875, Mary McLeod was the 15th child born to her former slave parents in Mayesville, South Carolina.

   As a Christian and a very spiritual person, she was determined to become a home mission teacher, so she left home to study at Scotia Seminary in Concord, North Carolina, and then went to Chicago to complete her studies at the Institute for Home and Foreign Mission.

   After marrying Albertus Bethune in her early twenties, having a child, and taking on other responsibilities as a mother and wife, she postponed her career plans.

   Eventually, she began to believe that she was being called to provide a higher education for African American youth in Florida. Her determination and deep faith resulted in the gradual establishment of present-day Bethune-Cookman College located in Daytona, Florida.

   Later in her life, because of her nationally recognized leadership, Mrs. Bethune was appointed to President Franklin D. Roosevelt's "Black Cabinet," and an advisor for the government's new National Youth Administration.

   She also became Vice-President of the NAACP, and helped found the National Council of Negro Women.

6. In 1896, the same year the U.S. Supreme Court made a decision upholding segregation in the *Plessy v. Ferguson* case, William Edward Burghart Du Bois was the first African American to earn a Ph.D. from Harvard University.

Today, Du Bois is considered to be one of Harvard's most outstanding graduates and scholars. His landmark Ph.D. dissertation, "The Suppression of the African Slave Trade" became the first volume in the yearly *Harvard Journal's* publications.

He is also considered one of America's leading social scientists, because of his research and considerable writing in the social sciences, particularly in sociology and its focus on participant observation in field studies.

As founding editor of the NAACP's "Crisis" magazine, Du Bois was able to clearly define and describe the nature of the harmful and unjust consequences of racism for African Americans, and how Congress and the succession of presidents did nothing to put an end to lynchings or to really protect the Constitutional rights of African Americans.

Today, "Crisis" magazine is still the official publication of the NAACP. It continues to build on Du Bois' literary legacy as one of the best organizational publications in the U.S., one which reaches thousands of readers and continues to focus mainly on civil rights issues as they affect all Americans.

Although Du Bois was the first African American to earn a Ph.D. from Harvard, in 1870, Richard Greener was the first African American ever to earn an undergraduate degree from Harvard. He had a successful career as an educator, worked in the U.S. Treasury Department, and also with the U.S. diplomatic service.

7. In 1909 Rev. Lawrence C. Jones founded the Piney Woods Country Life School on acreage about 20 miles from Jackson, Mississippi. Facing great odds, he gradually received support from a cross-section of donors.

From its inception to the present, the school offers a strong academic program with emphasis on basic learning skills, college and career preparation, agricultural and real life skills, and JROTC. Classes are taught from grades 9-12. Spirituality is also emphasized.

The school prides itself on providing quality academic and vocational education for more than 300 students. A high percentage of graduates attend and succeed at prestigious colleges throughout the country.

The Southern Association of Colleges and Schools and the National Association of Independent Schools accredit the school Piney Woods as a top rate preparatory school.

8. Benjamin E. Mays was born in Epworth, South Carolina, in 1895, and as a child he began to show his exceptional intellectual, speaking, and leadership abilities.

    Later, his teaching and administrative positions at South Carolina State and Howard University provided him with the necessary experience to become President of Morehouse College in Atlanta, Georgia, where he served from 1940 until 1967.

9. a. Dr. Ruth Love became the first woman Superintendent of Schools in Oakland, California, from 1975-81. She, with her administrative staff and teachers, introduced innovative academic and scholarship programs that helped many students attain higher national test scores. She had previously taught school in Oakland, and had worked for the California Department of Education and the Department of Education in Washington, D.C., where she was largely responsible for directing the federal government's Right to Read program.

    Love was appointed General Superintendent of Schools in Chicago where she served from 1981-85, the first woman to hold a position in such a large urban school district.

Through her visionary and dedicated leadership, she and others developed the Chicago Master Reading Learning Program, which became a solid and progressive foundation for improved student achievement throughout the district, and a model for other school districts.

Earlier in her career as a Fullbright Exchange Teacher and director of a Crossroads Africa humanitarian program in Africa, she became motivated to make a lifetime commitment to help improve the lives and education of people in Ghana, Africa. Today, through Ruth Love Enterprises, she is accomplishing that goal.

Recently, Dr. Love was the recipient of the 2005 Bishop Roy A. Nichols award for her outstanding leadership in giving direction to a grassroots community development project sponsored by the Downs Memorial United Methodist Church in Oakland, California. b. Dr. Betty Hopkins Mason first became a Superintendent of Schools in Gary, Indiana, in 1988. She faced the difficult task of not only improving students' basic reading, writing, and computing skills but doing it within the framework of a limited budget and resistance from some uncooperative school board members.

In 1993, she was officially appointed the first woman, and first African American, Superintendent of Schools in Oklahoma City. She had already been working in the capacity of acting superintendent since the fall of 1992.

Under her brief but successful administration, the Oklahoma School District had one of the largest bond measures ever passed, amounting to 89.9 million dollars. This enabled the district to reopen and renovate school facilities, adjust class sizes, and open an innovative new school program in visual and performing arts and international studies at one of its magnet schools.

One of the most challenging experiences in Dr. Mason's career took place during the trauma and aftermath of the terrorist bombing of the Alfred P. Murrah Federal Building in Oklahoma City in the spring of 1995.

Some family members, loved ones and friends of school district staff had been killed or severely injured in the blast. Fortunately, none of the children or staff at any of the schools had been injured. Dr. Mason and others had to immediately arrange for counseling of students and staff, and consoling family members and friends of those who had been victims of the bombing.

Although now retired, Dr. Mason continues to use her leadership skills on a volunteer basis to assist schools in Boley, Oklahoma, and currently as superintendent of St. John's Christian Academy in Oklahoma City.

She continues to receive much deserved recognition for her efforts as an educator and role model.

10. In 1968, Elizabeth Duncan Koontz was the first African American educator to be elected president of the National Education Association (NEA) after many years of active participation with the organization. She advocated close cooperation between school administrators, teachers, and parents in determining educational policy and curriculum development. In 1969, President Richard Nixon appointed her to direct the Women's Bureau of the Department of Labor.

Education has been, and is still, a primary value for African Americans in spite of the many years of institutional racism and segregation that prevented them from receiving it, especially quality education.

Initially, slaves were allowed to attain a limited level of literacy, but only for the purpose of being productive workers.

Gradually, some individual Christians and church groups provided limited literacy education for slaves and free African Americans. However, this was mainly done for the purpose of converting them to Christianity and to make them literate for reading and understanding the Bible.

However, after the Civil War, much of the initial phase of the educational programs to educate African Americans focused on providing mass literacy programs for the purpose of teaching all ages of the freed slaves how to read and write.

Young white teachers, and some African American young people, were recruited by various church groups to go to the South and work as educational missionaries.

After many years of growth and development, more than 100 colleges (HBCUs) were founded offering different educational programs related to academic learning and skills training in home economics, farming and other curricula.

Today, many of these schools are funded and staffed by African Americans. As a result, in the 21st century more and more African Americans than ever before are acquiring a level and quality of education and skills that enables them to freely pursue their career and life goals in the U.S. and throughout the world.

QUIZ 17 ANSWERS
Historical Black Colleges and Universities: A Brief Overview

1. Today, a "Historical Black College and University" re-
    fers to an accredited educational institution of higher
    learning that offers college level courses. Upon satis-
    factory completion of a prescribed course of study, the
    HBCU grants degrees at the undergraduate, masters,
    professional and doctoral levels.

    After the Civil War, the majority of HBCUs were
    founded as "institutes" and "normal" training schools
    for the education of promising African American
    youth. The goal was to educate and train a select group
    of African Americans who in turn would acquire the
    necessary knowledge and skills to help teach the ma-
    jority of the newly-freed slaves, young and old alike, to
    become literate and to learn various manual arts skills
    so that they could improve their lives and become eco-
    nomically self-sufficient.

2. Currently, there are 107 HBCUs enrolling more than 200,000 students of diverse social and economic backgrounds, and each year approximately 46,500 students earn undergraduate and graduate degrees from HBCUs.

   A combined total enrollment of about 20% of all African American college students are attending HBCU schools.

3. Most HBCUs are located in the Atlantic and Gulf coastal areas, and inland southern states.

   North Carolina has the largest number of HBCUs, followed by Georgia, Alabama, Louisiana, South Carolina, and 14 other states.

   They were founded in this part of the U.S. after the Civil War mainly because this is where the majority of freed African Americans slaves lived, and because of their eagerness to become educated.

4. Lincoln University, which is located near Philadelphia, Pennsylvania, grew out of Ashmun Institute, which was founded in 1854 and largely funded and supported by members of the Presbyterian Church.

   Three of its outstanding graduates are Thurgood Marshall, who became the first African American appointed to the U.S. Supreme Court as an Associate Justice in 1967; Kwame Nkrumah who became the first President of the Republic of Ghana in 1960; and Bishop Roy C. Nichols who became the first African American appointed as a Bishop in the United Methodist Church in 1968.

5. Howard University was first chartered as a seminary in 1867, and was founded as Howard Normal and Theological Institute for Education.

6. In 1868, at Hampton, Virginia, Hampton Normal and Agricultural Institute started mainly as a co-educational elementary and secondary school to educate a select group of African American and Native American youth.

Its principal, Samuel Armstrong, was a former Union Army officer and son of a Congregational missionary. Using his father's educational missionary work in Hawaii as a model, he placed emphasis on manual and industrial arts training.

Armstrong's efforts were successful and Hampton became a showcase for this kind of education at the time. Booker T. Washington, Armstrong's prize student, organized a similar program at Tuskegee.

Today, Hampton University is a highly rated academic institution in the U.S. and offers a broad range of undergraduate and graduate programs.

Its Honors College and Leadership Institute programs are nationally recognized as the result of having one of the most diverse distinguished faculties of any HBCUs in the U.S.

7. a. Martin Luther King, Jr. (1948).
   b. Maynard Jackson (1956).
   c. Julian Bond (1971).
   d. Samuel Jackson (1972).
   e. Spike Lee (1979).

Morehouse College was founded in Atlanta, GA in 1867, to provide higher education for exceptional African American males who showed great academic promise and leadership.

Since its beginning, Morehouse graduates have distinguished themselves in all walks of life. It is rated as one of the finest small colleges in the U.S., with an enrollment of more than 2,700 students.

Along with Spelman College in Atlanta, Morehouse was designated by "Black Enterprise" magazine to be one of the best colleges for African Americans to attend because of its academic program and professional leadership emphasis.

Currently, Dr. Walter T. Massey, formerly a well-respected administrator at the University of California, Berkeley, is president.

8. In the early 1940s, Tuskegee Army Airfield, located at Tuskegee Institute in Alabama, was selected to be the primary training center for the very first group of African American pilots in the history of the Army Air Force.

   They were eventually referred to as the "Tuskegee Airmen," but were officially designated the Ninety-ninth Fighter Pursuit Squadron.

   Two of America's first African American Air Force generals, Benjamin O. Davis, Jr., and Daniel "Chappie" James, got their training at Tuskegee Army Air Field.

   Founded in 1881, Tuskegee University currently enrolls 3000 students in undergraduate and graduate degree programs in more than 50 majors. It is the only HBCU that has a College of Veterinary Medicine that confers the Doctor of Veterinary Medicine professional degree.

9. a. In 1875, Alabama Agricultural and Mechanical University (AAMU), founded in Huntsville, AL, has 5,914 students.

b. Bethune-Cookman College, founded in Daytona Beach, Florida, in 1904, has 3000 students.

c. Dillard University, founded in 1869 in New Orleans, LA, has 2,225 students.

d. Florida Agricultural and Mechanical University (FAMU), founded in 1887 at Tallahassee, FL, has 12,465 students.

e. Jackson State University, founded in 1877 at Jackson, MS, has 7,783 students.

f. Johnson C. Smith University, founded in Charlotte, NC, in 1867, has 1,532 students.

g. Shaw University, founded in 1865 in Raleigh, NC, has 2,613 students.

h. Spelman College, founded in 1881 in Atlanta, GA, has 2,121 students.

i. Wilberforce University, founded at Wilberforce, Ohio, in 1856, has 1,190 students.

j. Xavier University, founded in 1925 at New Orleans, LA, has 3,994 students.

10. In addition to providing educational opportunities and career training for individual students, HBCUs have made significant contributions to the following aspects of American life, culture and society:

a. Helped to educate and prepare the majority of African American professionals (dentists, doctors, entertainers, judges, musicians, scientists, teachers and social workers, etc.).

b. Helped to provide leaders for business, civil rights, education, government, religion and many other American institutions.

c. Helped to influence the development of a viable substantial segment of America's middle class.

d. Helped to contribute to the education, leadership, and professional development of many non-African Americans who live in the West Indies, Africa, and other parts of the world.

e. Through college campus Reserve Officers' Training Corps have and continue to prepare many for military service, especially at the officer level.

EBONY OWL: DID YOU KNOW?

In the fall of 2001, nearly 30 Russian students, and 16 students from Algeria, Colombia, Ghana, and Turkey were attending Alcorn State University, a HBCU in southwest Mississippi. It has a predominantly African American student body of more than 3000 students, and academic and service programs that attract foreign students.

When the Russian students were asked why they chose to attend Alcorn, they responded that the school had an excellent reputation of meeting foreign students' academic and support service needs.

It is a known and established fact that many HBCUs are providing higher education on par with and in some cases superior to a number of the predominantly white colleges and universities.

Also, many HBCUs provide an educational environment that is very conducive to optimal student learning, and in many instances have a variety of support and counseling services beneficial to students that they might not receive at some large competitive schools.

1. Andrew Carnegie (1835-1919) and John D. Rockefeller, Jr. (1874-1960).

2. Julius Rosenwald (1862-1932), president of Sears, Roebuck and Company.

3. a. Howard Univ. — Congregational
   b. Johnson C. Smith Univ. — Presbyterian
   c. Lincoln Univ. — Methodist
   d. Morehouse College — Baptist
   e. Xavier — Catholic

4. Dr. Frederick Patterson of Tuskegee Institute founded the United Negro College Fund, Inc., (UNCF) and since its inception has raised more than $2.2 billion to assist students attending HBCUs.

5. Delta Sigma Theta Sorority.

6. John D. Rockefeller, Jr.

7. The Annenberg Foundation, the Bill and Melinda Gates Foundation, Exxon Education Foundation, Johnson Publishing Company, and Oprah Winfrey Foundation.

8. Drs. Bill and Camille Cosby have donated more than $20 million to support HBCUs and other institutions of higher learning in the U.S. for many years.

9. Lou Rawls, who closed the annual fundraiser by saying, "A mind is a terrible thing to waste."

10.a. Jackie Joyner-Kersee Community Foundation.
   b. Jack and Jill of America Foundation.
   c. Michael Jordan Foundation.
   d. Links, Inc.
   e. Jackie Robinson Foundation.
   f. Dionne Warwick Foundation.
   g. Harold Washington Foundation.
   h. Doug Williams Foundation.
   i. David Winfield Foundation.

In 1944 when the first UNCF National Council fundraising campaign was started, it was endorsed and chaired by millionaire and Baptist John D. Rockefeller, Jr., who held the voluntary position for 15 years.

The DeWitt Wallace Fund, a foundation fund originally established by the Reader's Digest *publication, bestowed a thirty-seven million dollar endowment gift to Spelman College, an HBCU. in Atlanta, Georgia, in 1992. It is one of the largest amounts ever given to any single HBCU.*

It should be noted that each year, throughout the nation, many colleges and universities receive and utilize alumni and endowment funds to finance their programs, including HBCUs.

Also, it is not well known that many African American church groups organize annual fund raising activities to give thousands of dallars in scholarship money to students in their own churches as well as to other education scholarship funds.

1. Paul Cuffe (1759-1817).

2. James Forten (1766-1842).

3. Maggie Lena Walker (1867-1934).

4. Madame C.J. Walker (1867-1919).

5. William Leidesdorff (1810-1848).

6. Lydia Flood Jackson (1862-?).

7. Jake Simmons, Jr. (1901-1981).

8. Charles Clinton Spaulding (1874-1952).

9. Arthur George Gaston (1892-1996).

10. Oprah Winfrey was born January 29, 1954, in the small, economically impoverished town of Kosciusko, Mississippi.

After moving to Nashville, Tennessee, she began training in the performing arts and public speaking, and became good at both. Eventually, this led to her doing very popular news and talk shows in Baltimore and Chicago.

This success enabled her to launch her own one-hour "Oprah Winfrey Show" in 1985, which since its inception has been awarded the Daytime Emmy Award for best talk show on television and has begun its 20th television season.

She has also had a very successful acting career in such movies as: "The Color Purple" and "Brewster Place."

Among her many contributions to charitable causes are large donations to support the Family for Better Lives Foundation, the Oprah Winfrey Foundation, and to Tennessee State University, her alma mater. Also, her generous philanthropy benefits people all around the world, especially children.

She also created the Oprah Winfrey Book Club that has encouraged increased reading on a variety of topics, and at the same time has featured authors who ordinarily may not get exposure to the public.

Currently, Oprah is not only one of the wealthiest

Americans, but she is also one of the ten most popular and influential woman television personalities in the U.S. She not only has considerable financial power as CEO of Harpo (Oprah spelled backwards) Incorporated and Harpo Entertainment Group, but in this capacity she is credited with having helped a number of persons in the entertainment industry, including Dr. Phil's TV talk show.

One of America's great poet laureates, Dr. Maya Angelou, comments that Oprah Winfrey is a "phenomenal woman!" Oprah's motto is: "God gives to those who give."

EBONY OWL: DID YOU KNOW?

It has only been in the latter part of the 20th century that African Americans have had greater opportunities to expand their entrepreneurial efforts and become more integrally involved in the free enterprise system of the U.S. economy.

Consequently there are a significant number of African Americans in the middle, upper-middle, and upper socio/economic classes of America.

Equal opportunity legislation beginning in the 1960s, and various private and public affirmative action policies essentially helped to bring about this change; a change that has not only benefited African Americans but also the country as a whole.

However, it has been the education, ingenuity, and abilities of many individual African Americans and their own home-grown organizations that have contributed to the significant economic progress and accumulation of wealth for an increasing number of persons in this population.

It also must be kept in mind that as a group of many millions, African Americans have not had access to significnt amounts of financial resources and support outside of the U.S., as has been and still is the case for some immigrant groups coming to America in latter decades of the 20th century.

Therefore, because of this important difference, the economic progress of African Americans ought not be compared or measured by what is considerred to be progress in those groups, whose populations and socio-economic backgrounds are quite different.

1. Hiram Rhoades Revels and Blanche Kelso Bruce were the first two African Americans to serve in the U.S. Senate. During the Reconstruction period both were elected senators to represent the state of Mississippi, Revels in 1870 and Bruce in 1874.

BLANCHE KELSO BRUCE

   Ironically, Revels had filled Jefferson Davis' vacant seat in the Senate when Davis left to become the president of the South's Confederate States of America.

2. A total of 14 were elected and appointed to serve in the Reconstruction Congress largely because of the disfranchisement of white southern politicians who had supported the Confederacy.

   For the most part they were not experienced politicians but were ordinary laymen. For example, in 1870, Joseph Hayne Rainey, a former barber, and Robert Smalls, a naval hero during the Civil War, were elected to represent South Carolina in the U.S House of Representatives. All of the representatives were Republicans.

3. In 1871-72, Pinckney B.S. Pinchbach, an active African American Republican politician in Louisiana, first became lieutenant governor, and then acting governor as the result of statutory lines of succession.

4. Langston, Oklahoma, and Langston University, located about 50 miles northeast of Oklahoma City, are named after John Mercer Langston, a former Virginia slave.

He eventually was educated at Oberlin College, was a lawyer and became first dean of Howard University's Law Department.

Langston was appointed to a number of federal government positions, and was elected to Congress in 1889 representing the state of Virginia.

Langston town and Langston University were given his name to commemorate his exceptional achievements as an educator, politician, U.S. government official, and humanitarian.

Langston Hughes was born in 1902 in Joplin, Missouri, and was given the first name "Langston," to honor both his grandfather, Charles Langston, a noted politician, and his nationally known grand-uncle, John Mercer Langston.

5. a. Lawrence Douglas Wilder became the first African American in the 20th century to be elected to the position of lieutenant governor in 1985 and governor in 1991 in Virginia.

He was educated at two HBCU's: Virginia Union University and Howard University. He was awarded the Bronze Star for his meritorious service during the Korean War, and was very successful in working his way up through Virginia political ranks to eventually become governor.

b. Columbus City Councilwoman Jeanette Bradley was elected Ohio's lieutenant governor; attorney Michael Steele was elected Maryland's lieutenant governor. Both are Republicans.

6. a. In 1968, Shirley Chisholm (1924-2005) was the first African American woman to be elected to the U.S. House of Representatives for New York. Prior to this she had been a New York state legislator.

Shirley Chisholm was also the first American woman to seek the office of President of the U.S. She did so as a candidate for the Democratic Party in 1972.

b. Barbara Jordan became one of the most eloquent and effective speakers in Congress, and at the 1992 Democratic National Convention she was selected to be the keynote speaker, nominating Bill Clinton for President.

She began her political career in 1966, when she was the first African American woman to be elected as a state senator in Texas, and the first to be elected to the Texas House of Representatives in 1972.

SHIRLEY CHISOLM

7. a. In 1966, Edward Brooke was elected to the U.S. Senate for Massachusetts and served thirteen years.

b. In 1992, Carole Moseley-Braun became the first African American woman to be elected to the U.S. Senate for Illinois.

Both Brooke and Mosley-Braun were lawyers before being elected to the Senate. Brooke was Attorney General of Massachusetts, and Moseley-Braun worked with the U.S Attorney General in Illinois.

c. Former Illinois State Senator Barack Obama was elected in November 2004, to the U.S. Senate, making him only the third African American to serve in that body of the federal government since Reconstruction.

Currently, 39 African Americans serve in the House of Representatives, and one, Barak Obama, in the U.S. Senate,

CAROL MOSELY-BRAUN

8. a. Maynard Jackson of Atlanta in 1973.

   b. Harold Washington of Chicago in 1873.

   c. Coleman Young of Detroit in 1973.

   d. Richard Hatcher of Gary in 1967.

   e. Carrie S. Perry of Hartford in 1987.

   f. Tom Bradley of Los Angeles in 1773.

   g. Sharon S. Belton of Minneapolis in 1994.

   h. Kenneth Gibson of Newark in 1970.

   i. David Dinkins of New York in 1989.

   j. Willie Brown of San Francisco in 1996.

9. a. President Lyndon B. Johnson appointed Robert Weaver to serve as Secretary of Housing and Urban Development.

   b. President Jimmy Carter appointed Patricia R. Harris to serve as Secretary of Health and Human Services, and Clifford Alexander to serve as Secretary of the Army.

   c. President William J. Clinton appointed Mike Espy as Secretary of Agriculture, Hazel R. O'Leary as Secretary of Energy, and Ronald H. Brown as Secretary of Commerce.

10. Congresswoman Barbara Lee, in the U.S. House of Representatives for the 9th District in Northern California, had, and still has, broad support from her constituents and many others throughout the nation for the stand she has taken regarding the U.S. waging war in Iraq.

EBONY OWL: DID YOU KNOW?

Historically, after the Civil War when African Americans gained the right to vote, they affiliated with the Republican Party. This was due mainly to the fact that Abraham Lincoln was a Republican, and that he and other Republicans were considered to be responsible for abolishing slavery and for enacting legislation to give African Americans their full citizenship rights.

However, political party affiliation with the Republican Party began to radically change for African Americans with the election and executive actions of President Franklin D. Roosevelt and subsequent Democratic Party presidents.

As a matter of fact, in 1928, Oscar DePriest, a Republican, was the one and only African American in the U.S. House of Represen-

tatives for many decades. Many African Americans soon felt that the Republican Party was not as responsive to their needs as Democrats, so many switched parties.

Beginning in the 1990s, there began a gradual trend that indicates African Americans in some parts of the U.S., including the South, are affiliating once again with the Republican party for various reasons. Some political pundits relate this to the party's new recruiting efforts, and the position it takes on such issues as abortion, gay rights, and other conservative political issues.

It is also interesting to note that in the early years of the 21st century there are hundreds of African Americans who have been elected and appointed to more governmental positions in the South than in any other region of the U.S. These persons have affiliations with both major political parties.

QUIZ 21 ANSWERS

The NAACP, National Urban League, and Other Civil Rights and Community Organizations: A Brief Overview

1. In 1909, the National Association for the Advancement of Colored People (NAACP) was formally established in New York City, mainly by a group of prominent white Americans.

   Their main purpose was to create an interracial, proactive organization whose main agenda would be to bring about full citizenship for African Americans and to get the U.S. Congress to pass legislation to outlaw lynchings.

   Among those white Americans who established the NAACP were pioneering social workers Jane Addams and Mary White Ovington, newspaper publishers Oswald Garrison Villard and William English Walling.

   Influential African Americans included educator W.E.B. Du Bois, journalist Ida B. Wells, and clergymen William Henry Brooks and Alexander Walters.

   The NAACP is one of the oldest and most broadly representative civil rights organizations in the U.S. and one of the most effective in protecting citizenship rights not only for African Americans but for all

Americans.

Today, the NAACP's basic mission is to actively advocate for, and take action to protect, the civil rights of individuals and groups who have been denied those rights, regardless of race, creed or color. Its national membership of more than one half million reflects this kind of diversity.

As a non-profit organization, it relies mainly on contributions from individual members, various organizations, and corporations. College students also organize themselves into NAACP chapters.

Thousands of dedicated volunteers also work in various capacities to implement its goals and objectives, and to provide leadership for its programs.

In addition, there are highly experienced professional lawyers and other experts within and outside of the organization who assist on a free *pro bono* basis. They work through local branch and regional offices.

Since 1910, the official publication of the NAACP has been "Crisis" magazine. It was created by Dr. W.E.B. Du Bois and through the years has been a critical and thought-provoking medium dealing with various civil rights issues and challenges confronting African Americans locally and nationally. It has a broad circulation not only to NAACP members but to other interested persons as well. It continues to represent one of the best examples of quality journalism in the U.S.

NAACP's "ACT-SO" is a relatively new youth-oriented program that is very successful. It has ongoing academic, community service, and cultural enrichment programs designed to encourage, enhance the abilities, and increase the involvement of African American youth in grades 9 through 12. ACT-SO is an acronym for Academic, Cultural, Technological, and Scientific Olympics. Each year thousands of youth participate and benefit from this non-profit program in many parts of the U.S. The former CEO of Verizon Communications is the current Executive Secretary of the NAACP, Mr. Bruce Gordon.

2. The National Urban League (NUL) was initially organized in 1911 by Fisk University sociologists George E. Haynes and Eugene K. Jones for the main purpose of bringing about equal opportunities in employment and economic opportunities, and other citizenship rights, for African Americans, especially for those living in the South.

As a 21st-century non-profit, nonpartisan and inter-racial organization, it has expanded its mission to also include making periodic reports on various aspects of the economic status of African Americans compared to the majority population of Americans and certain other ethnic groups. As a result of its scientific and statistical data, both private and public institutions often rely on its findings as a reference to determine their policies and programs.

From the beginning, the leadership of the National Urban League has benefited from exceptional men and women with outstanding educational and professional backgrounds whether as members of the NUL board of trustees or as executive directors. To name a few: Lester Granger, Whitney Young, Vernon Jordan, and the current director, Marc Morial.

3. In 1942, James Farmer took the lead in organizing the Congress of Racial Equality (CORE) as a biracial civil rights organization. Its main purpose was to take non-violent direct action to challenge institutional racism, segregation, and discrimination in major facets of American society. Economic boycotts of department stores like Montgomery Ward, restaurant "sit-ins," and bus "freedom rides" were techniques of direct action that were often used to bring about desired change.

Besides Farmer, Bayard Rustin was a very effective and influential field secretary and organizer for the organization for many years, and in 1968, Roy E. A.

Innis became the national director.

4. In 1960, the Student Nonviolent Coordinating Committee (SNCC) was organized by Dr. Martin L. King, Jr., and African Americans students from Shaw University and other nearby HBCUs.

    They were trained and coached in how to use nonviolent techniques such as "sit-ins" in order to desegregate restaurants and other kinds of accommodations.

5. In 1957, after bombings of African American churches in Montgomery, Alabama, by white racists, the Southern Christian Leadership Conference (SCLC) was organized by a denominational cross-section of clergy and lay church members. Its main purpose and objectives were to seek and take active nonviolent steps to bring about first-class rights for African Americans in the South and throughout the country. Dr. Martin L. King, Jr., was elected president, and Rev. Ralph David Abernathy was elected secretary-treasurer.

6. In 1966, Huey P. Newton and Bobby Seale, college students in Oakland, California, organized the Black Panther Party (BPP).

It was created largely in response to racial profiling, police harassment, and what was considered to be the blatant oppression and neglect of the African American community in the city of Oakland.

BPP leader Eldridge Cleaver's book, "Soul on Ice," written in earthy and plain talk language, clearly described many of the underlying social conditions of many African Americans that gave rise to the BPP.

The BPP agenda also emphasized armed self-defense and involvement in volunteer community self-help programs in African American inner cities. For example, Black Panther neighborhood centers were set up to feed impoverished children and to provide tutoring, free clothing, and food. Housing programs for the homeless were also provided.

In 1974, Elaine Brown became chairperson of the BPP and was a key leader for the organization.

7. In 1914, Marcus Garvey organized the Universal Negro Improvement Association (UNIA) in Jamaica, his country of birth.

   After moving to New York City, a branch was organized there in 1916, and in less than five years gained a large membership in many parts of the country.

   It called on all people of African ancestry to unify their efforts to improve their economic, political and social conditions worldwide.

   Reclaiming colonized African lands, and renewing pride in Africa's glorious cultural past was also part the organization's agenda.

8. In 1925, Asa Philip Randolph took the lead in organizing the Brotherhood of Sleeping Car Porters and Maids (BSCP). However, it wasn't until 1937 that BSCP became an effective collective bargaining union. In that year some eight thousand Pullman Company porters, maids, and cooks received substantial increases in wages.

   In 1941 the union was also successful in influencing U.S. President Franklin D. Roosevelt to create the Fair Employment Practices Committee (FEPC) in order to end employment discrimination in World War II defense industries (war production industries) against African Americans.

9. In 1784-87, Prince Hall, a free person from Barbados and an American Revolutionary war patriot, was finally granted a charter directly from the British Grand Lodge in England to form the Masonic African Lodge No. 459 in Boston, Massachusetts. Lodge 459 became the first independent African American Masonic organization in the U.S.

Earlier, Hall and a group of other African Americans sought to be sponsored by their white American counterpart, but were denied.

Eventually, they became known as Prince Hall Masons, and for many years the group has served its members and the larger community in many ways.

10. In 1906, seven male students who were enrolled at Cornell University in Ithaca, N.Y, started the oldest African American Greek-letter fraternity in the U.S., Alpha Phi Alpha (APA).

With help from a very small community of African Americans living in Ithaca, a house was secured off-campus where the students would have a place to stay. Prior to this, they were repeatedly denied housing on Cornell's campus, and discriminated against in other ways even though they were students enrolled at the school.

Since its inception the fraternity's principles have

focused on excellence in academics, good character, community service, and spiritual values.

Today, the non-profit Alpha Phi Alpha Fraternity, Inc., is made up of hundreds of college and alumni chapters with a membership of more than 175,000 in the U.S. and throughout the world.

Through its organizational structure, millions of dollars have been raised and donated to help students, academic institutions and community organizations.

Fraternity members have included such outstanding leaders as W.E.B. Du Bois, Paul Robeson, Thurgood Marshall, and Martin Luther King, Jr.

Two years after the APA was established African American female students at Howard University founded the Alpha Kappa Alpha Greek-letter sorority in 1908.

It stressed academic excellence, member loyalty, mutual aid, and community service, and currently it has a membership of more than 170,000 in the U.S., Caribbean, Africa and Europe.

Each year Alpha Phi Alpha and Alpha Kappa Alpha give thousands of dollars in scholarship funds to college students and help to provide them with different kinds of academic, guidance, and counseling support services.

There are also many other active African American Greek-letter sororities and fraternities on HBCU campuses. Among them are Kappa Alpha Psi, Omega Psi Phi, Phi Beta Sigma and Zeta Phi Beta, to name a few. With the assistance of alumni they are quite viable and help to provide different kinds of valuable support to students.

Another large and very influential sorority is the Delta Sigma Theta Sorority, Inc., comprising more than 190,000 college-educated women. It is currently organized in 870 chapters worldwide which provide scholarships to promote quality education and support human service programs.

Although not a sorority, The Links, Inc., is an outstanding community service organization made up of more than 10,000 professional women organized in 472 chapters in 42 states and three countries abroad.

In addition to being successful role models, they are involved in a range of community programs as mentors, activists and volunteers who work in purposeful service. For some years, they have encouraged organ, tissue, and bone marrow donations in the African American community.

In one of his early writings ("Souls of Black Folk") W.E.B. Du Bois wrote one of the most definitive and clearest statements about the personal and group identity of African Americans:

"One ever feels his two-ness, — an American, a Negro; two thoughts, two unreconciled strivings; two warring ideals in one dark body, whose dogged strength alone keeps it from being torn asunder...."

Although Du Bois expressed his views a century ago, there are many African Americans living in 21st-century America who would agree with him to a considerable degree.

Many would say that such things as the legacy of racism and institutional discrimination expressed by racial profiling, disparities in employment, educational, and housing opportunities is evidence that a common "gut-level" and "heart-level" Americanism is yet to be experienced by a sizable number of African Americans.

QUIZ 22 ANSWERS
Talented and Exceptional Early Writers, Poets, Journalists and Artists

1. Phillis Wheatley (1753-1784).

2. David Walker (1785-1830), "Walker's Appeal."

3. Samuel Cornish (ca.1795-1859) and John Brown Russwurm (1799-1851) founded and published the first African American newspaper in 1827 in New York City.

    Cornish became minister of the first African American Presbyterian Church in New York City.

    Russwurm was one of the first African American college graduates in the U.S. when he graduated from Maine's Bowdoin College in 1826.

4. Frederick Douglass (1817-1895).

5. Mifflin Wister Gibbs (1823-1915).

6. Delilah Leontium Beasley (1871-1934).

7. Ida Bell Wells-Barnett (1862-1931).

8. Gwendolyn Brooks (1917-) for poetry, and Moneta Sleet, Jr., (1929-) for photography.

9. a. Mary Edmonia ("Wildfire") Lewis (1845-1890).
   b. Louis Mailou Jones (1913-2005).

10. Henry Ossawa Tanner (1859-1937).

For many decades after the Civil War there was a tremendous increase in African American controlled newspapers being published in different parts of the country, especially in urban areas.

Many of these 500 plus papers focused attention on issues of racism and related social, economic, and political issues involving employment, housing, lynchings in the South, and disfranchisement. They also served as important information and education sources for the people in local communities as well as vital instruments advocating real-life concerns. The "Philadelphia Tribune," "Chicago Defender," "Pittsburgh Courier," "Amsterdam News," and "Atlanta Daily Word," are examples of such powerful newspapers.

Today, as is the case for many mainstream media, the growing trends in multi-media competition for African American subscribers, the decrease in purely race issues, and the increase in Internet information sources has resulted in a dramatic decline in readership in a number of these papers.

QUIZ 23 ANSWERS

Inspiring and Joy-Giving Vocalists, Musicians and Entertainers

1. Thomas Greene Bethune (1849-1903).

2. In 1871, the Fisk Jubilee Singers, a group of students from recently established Fisk University, began concert tours to raise funds for their school. Their melodious renditions of slave songs and Negro spirituals attracted large crowds in the U.S. and Europe. As a result, they not only raised money to support their school, but also to help build the four-story Fisk Hall, one of the main buildings on the campus.

3. James Bland (1854-1911) wrote "Carry Me Back to Old Virginny," which oficially became the state song in 1940. He wrote hundreds of other songs, among them "Oh Dem Golden Slippers."

4. William Christopher "W.C." Handy, (1873-1958), "St.Louis Blues" and "Memphis Blues."

5. Bessie Smith (1894-1937), "Empress of the Blues"; Sarah Vaughan (1924-1990), "Mother of the Blues"; and Ella Fitzgerald (1917-1996), "First Lady of Song."

6. Paul Robeson (1898-1976).

7. Marian Anderson (1902-1993).

8. Edward Kennedy "Duke" Ellington (1899-1974), "Do Nothing Till You Hear From Me," and "Don't Get Around Much Anymore."

9. Mahalia Jackson (1911-1972).

10. Daniel Louis "Satchmo" Armstrong (1900-1971), "Hello Dolly."

African American music is home grown. It has some African roots, but most of it comes from a whole range of experiences involving rejection, hostility, and even violence; but more importantly is overshadowed by a sense of dignity and love of justice and humanity.

American culture has been greatly enriched by talented and ingenious music and entertainment artists, especially during the 20th century.

QUIZ 24 ANSWERS

*Record-Breaking African American Athletes
and Sports Champions in the U.S.
and the World*

1. Isaac "Ike" Burns Murphy (1861-1896), whose father was a slave, set a record of winning 628 races out of 1412 professional horse races, including riding and winning three Kentucky Derby champion horses: Buchanan in 1884, Riley in 1890 and Kingman in 1891.

   Murphy's professional race horseriding feats were almost lost to horseracing history until 1967, when he was finally given a prominent burial monument at Man O' War Park in Lexington, Kentucky. He is also recognized in the Kentucky Derby Hall of Fame.

2. Mamie "Peanuts" Johnson (1936-).

3. a. Jack "Jackie" Roosevelt Robinson (1919-1971) for the Brooklyn Dodgers. In 1962, he was inducted into the Baseball Hall of Fame.

   b. Larry Doby (1924-2003) for the Cleveland Indians in 1947. He was voted into the Baseball Hall of Fame in 1998.

4. Frank Robinson (1935-), who began managing the Cleveland Indians in 1974, and Cito Gaston (1944-), who managed the Toronto Blue Jays team that won the World Series in 1992 and 1993.

5. a. John Arthur "Jack" Johnson (1878-1946), portrayed by James Earl Jones.
b. Joseph Louis Barrow or "Joe Louis," the "Brown Bomber" (1914-1981), who defeated Max Schmeling.
c. Muhammad Ali (1942-). Five of his notable achievements are:

a. In 1960, he won an Olympic Gold Medal in heavyweight competition representing the U.S.

b. In 1964, he won the heavyweight title from Sonny Liston.

c. Although he was stripped of his boxing title and barred from his profession after his refusal to be drafted in the U.S. Army in 1967, he was later vindicated by the courts.

d. In 1974, he defeated George Foreman in Zaire, Africa, and regained his title.

e. In 1978, he lost to Leon Spinks, but won back his title the next year.

6. a. James Cleveland "Jesse" Owens (1913-1980).
    b. Wilma Rudolph (1940-1994).

7. a. Arthur Ashe (1943-1993).
    b. Althea Gibson (1927).

8. Wilt Chamberlain (1936-2003), who played with the Philadelphia Warriors in 1961-62. Bill Russell, who began managing the Boston Celtics in 1966.

9. a. Marion Motley for the Cleveland Browns in 1947, and Fletcher Joe Perry for the San Francisco 49ers in 1948. Both played in the fullback position.
    b. After playing nine seasons with the Cleveland Browns, Jim Brown earned recognition as the greatest running back in the National Football League, where he rushed for 12,312 yards and made 126 touchdowns during the late 1950s. He was the first African American football player to receive the NFL's Most Valuable Player award in 1963, and in 1971, he was elected to NFL Hall of Fame.

    Today, Emmitt Smith, formerly playing with the Dallas Cowboys, and recently retiring from the Arizona Cardinals, holds the top records for a running back in the NFL. In a 15-year career he ran for a record 18,355 yards and made 164 touchdowns.

10. Milt Campbell won the Olympic decathlon in 1956 at Melbourne, Australia, with a new record of 7,937 points, and in 1958, Rafer Johnson won the decathlon in Moscow, Russia, with a new record of 8,302 points.

EBONY OWL – DID YOU KNOW?

Although many outstanding African American athletes actively participate in professional baseball, basketball, and football sports, only a very small number are actually hired as coaches and managers

For example, in the National Football League (NFL) there are only five head coaches: Tony Dungy of the Indianapolis Colts, Herman Edwards of the New York Jets, Marvin Lewis with the Cincinnati Bengals, Danny Green, who formerly coached the Minnesota Vikings, is head coach with the Arizona Cardinals, and recently, Romeo Crennel, defensive coordinator for 2005 Super Bowl champions New England Patriots, has been hired as head coach of the Cleveland Browns.

From the earliest years beginning in the late 1940s to the present, African American professional athletes have taken an effec-

tive proactive stand to do away with institutional discrimination in professional sports.

As a result, at no other time in U.S. professional sports history have such a considerable number of African American professional athletes begun to earn salaries and signed financial contracts on par with their white counterparts.

Wilma Rudolph

QUIZ 25 ANSWERS

African Americans Who Are Commemorated On United States Postage Stamps

1. In 1940, Booker T. Washington was commemorated because of his outstanding educational leadership at Tuskeegee Institute in Alabama.

2. In 1985, Mary McLeod Bethune, because of her push for civil rights in Washington, D.C., her work as an educator in Florida, her humanitarian work, and her appointment as a special delegate to the initial founding of the United Nations in San Francisco.

3. In 1984, a U.S. postage stamp was issued to commemorate the efforts of Dr. Carter G. Woodson to successfully promote and institute "Negro History," which is now observed nationally as "African American History Month" in February each year.

4. Harriet Tubman, the courageous and cunning Underground Railroad heroine, was recognized on a U.S. postage stamp in 1978.

5. Bessie Coleman.

6. Ralph Bunche in 1982.

7. Roy Wilkins in 2001.

8. Bill Pickett in 1994.

9. Billie Holiday, "Ma" Rainey, and Bessie Smith.

10. Martin Luther King, Jr.

EBONY OWL: DID YOU KNOW?

The U.S. Postal Service has issued more than seventy stamps commemorating the outstanding achievements of African Americans.

This recognition of noteworthy African Americans by the Postal Service didn't take place on a consistant basis until the latter decades of the 20th century. By this time, there was increasing factual information coming from African American studies at various universities chronicling the lives and accomplishments of these persons.

QUIZ 26 ANSWERS
Notable 20th Century African American Armed Services Heroes and Leaders

1. Dorie Miller (1919-1943).

2. The 761st Tank Battalion.

3. Benjamin O. Davis, Sr., (1877-1970) and Benjamin O. Davis, Jr. (1913-2003).

4. The 99th Pursuit Squadron or "Tuskegee Airmen."

5. Daniel "Chappie" James (1920-1978).

6. More than 4000 served in the U.S. and abroad.

7. a. In 1979, Hazel Johnson became the first to be commissioned a Brigadier General in the U.S. Army, serving in the Army Nurse Corps.
b. In 1990, Marcelite Harris was promoted to Brigadier General in the U.S. Air Force. She was assigned to command positions in Oklahoma and Texas.

---

8. In 1971, Samuel Gravely, Jr. (1922-2004) was the first African American ever to be promoted to Rear Admiral in the history of the U.S. Navy.

He started his naval career with the U.S. Naval Reserve, and during thirty years of service in WW II, the Korean, and Vietnam Wars, he achieved a distinguished and meritorious record while in command of various types of naval vessels.

9. J. Paul Reason was born in Washington D.C. and reared by parents who were well-known educators in the District's public schools and at Howard University.

As a 1965 graduate of the U.S. Naval Academy, he worked himself up through the ranks, taking on such responsibilities as Operations Officer, Electrical Officer, and Executive Officer on different types of naval ships.

From late 1976 until mid-1979, he was Naval Aide to President Jimmy Carter.

He served with distinction as commanding officer on a number of destroyers, nuclear guided missile cruisers, and aircraft carriers.

Ultimately, he became commander of the U.S. Atlantic Fleet, and the first African American four-star Admiral appointed in the U.S. Navy in 1996.

10. In 1979, Frank E. Petersen, Jr., was promoted to Brigadier General in the U.S. Marine Corps, and ten years later earned the rank of Lieutenant General.

His career began in 1952 after training at the Marine flying base at El Toro, California; he received his wings at Pensacola, Florida.

He flew 64 combat missions during the Korean War, and commanded a fighter squadron in Vietnam. He was awarded the Distinguished Flying Cross and many other medals for his outstanding service.

EBONY OWL: DID YOU KNOW?

African Americans have served and fought in every U.S. military conflict beginning with the American Revolution despite the fact that up until the 1950s they were required to serve in racially segregated units and usually denied equal opportunity and fair treatment in assignments and promotions.

Despite the racist attitudes and continued opposition before the desegregation of the Armed Services by President Harry S. Truman in 1948, African Americans have served the nation as patriots, and many of them, like others in the military, have been true heroines and heroes.

Today, it is to the credit of the U.S. Armed Services institutionalized affirmative action policies and programs that African Americans, as well as others, have been provided with equal opportunity to pursue their particular goals in the services. One of best examples of this having happened is to take a brief look at the career of retired four-star general Colin Powell.

Born in Harlem, New York, in 1937 and starting his preparatory career by becoming an officer in his college ROTC program at City College in New York, he became an officer in the regular army during the Vietnam War. For valor and bravery there, after two tours of duty and receiving the Purple Heart, he eventually earned and was promoted to higher officer ranks, culminating in a four-star general rank.

In 1989, President George H. W. Bush, father of President George W. Bush, appointed Colin Powell Chairman of the Joint Chiefs of Staff. This position gave him great responsibility as leader of all of the U. S. Armed Services. It also meant that during *the Gulf War of 1991, he had the ultimate responsibility under the president. No other African American had ever held this position of leadership for the nation.*

After many years as a dedicated military officer and exemplary patriotic American, Colin Powell accepted the challenge in 2000 to serve as Secretary of State under President George W. Bush.

Unfortunately, Powell's untarnished career in the military did not spare him criticism regarding the position he took for the administration regarding "weapons of mass destruction" in Iraq. Today, his credibility as a worldwide trusted leader with a level head and intelligent judgment has been greatly tarnished by the U.S. government's flawed intelligence reports regarding Iraq, reports that became the basis for a costly U.S. military invasion of Iraq in March of 2003.

QUIZ 27 ANSWERS

Time-Honored Celebrations and Cultural Observances

1. During the month of February, because it coincides with Abraham Lincoln's birthday on the 12th (1809), and Frederick Douglass' birthday on February 14th (1817).

2. Carter G. Woodson, a Ph.D. graduate from Harvard University and lifelong educator, is recognized as the prime mover to establish "Negro History Week," in 1926.

    Earlier, in 1915, he and others organized The Association for the Study of Negro Life and History (ASNLH). Its main purpose was, and still is today, to teach and educate African Americans and others about the true history and cultural roots of African Americans.

    In 1916 Woodson started a very scholarly publication, "Journal of Negro History." Today, it is published under the title, "Journal of African American History."

    In 1922, he also published "The Negro in Our History," one of the first textbooks used in African American schools for many years.

3. In 1900, James Weldon Johnson (1871-1938), a poet and writer, wrote the lyrics to "Lift Every Voice and Sing." His brother, J. Rosamond Johnson, composed the music.

Eventually, the song gained popularity and was referred to as the "Negro National Anthem." It was often sung at various organizational gatherings of African Americans, as it still is today, especially during African American History Month observances.

4. The "Negro National Flag" symbol or banner was popularized at the 1920 Universal Negro Improvement Association convention proceedings in New York. The color red stands for the blood of African people nobly shed in the past and dedicated to the future; black stands for pride in one's color of skin; and the color green stands for a new and better Africa.

5. "Juneteenth" refers to the historical celebration of slaves in some parts of the country who didn't learn about President Abraham Lincoln's executive order freeing slaves (The Emancipation Proclamation), until many months after January 1863.

   When they did, they rejoiced and celebrated, and today, there are "Juneteenth" celebrations and programs observed at different times by many descendants of African American slaves throughout the U.S., and especially in Texas, Florida and California.

6. Almost twenty years after his assassination, Dr. Martin Luther King, Jr.'s, birthday, which is on January 15, was officially observed as a national holiday on January 20, 1986.

   It is now observed the 3rd Monday of January each year. This was the first time in U.S. history that an African American citizen, or any American citizen who was not president, received such an honor.

   Dr. King was recognized nationally and internationally as one of the world's greatest civil rights leaders and proponents of non-violence, peace and social justice.

7. Malcolm X was born on May 19, 1925, and given the birth name Malcolm Little.

   Although he was assassinated February 21, 1965, various African American groups annually celebrate his life and his message of pride, power and community unity during the month of May.

8. "Kwanzaa" is an African Swahili language word that means "first fruits."

   In 1966, Maulana Karenga, a graduate philosophy student at the University of California, Los Angeles, conceived of the idea to start an end-of-the-year celebration that would be especially meaningful to all African Americans, and place emphasis on spiritual values and principles.

   It begins on December 26 and continues for seven days through January 1, each calendar year.

9. The seven spiritual principles that are observed sequentially, one each day, are as follows:
   a. Umoja = unity
   b. Kujichagulia = self-determination
   c. Ujima = collective work and responsibility
   d. Ujamaa = cooperative economics
   e. Nia = purpose
   f. Kuumba = creativity
   g. Imani = faith

   Each principle gives focus to a wide range of meaningful individual, family, and group activities throughout the seven-day Kwanzaa celebration period.

10. "Ramadan" is an Arabic word that refers to an annual religious observance required for all Muslims, including African American Muslims.
    Devout Muslims are expected to fast and to be abstinent from dawn to dusk each day for a month. The purpose is to enhance one's spirituality and focus on religious duties as a Muslim. It is observed in the ninth month of the Muslim lunar calendar, which is usually in the month of October.

Today, African Americans observe tradition-al American family and cultural events such as birthdays, weddings, gradua-tions, retirements, funerals, family re-unions, and national holidays just like other Americans.

However, in addition to their involvement in these common American cultural ac-tivities, many participate in programs and activities closely related to African American community life itself such as sorority and fraternal organizations, re-ligious institutions, book fairs, museums, community and business organizations, non-profits, travel tours, and educational programs, to name some. These can be lo-cal, regional, and national in focus and scope depending on the sponsor.

Finally, the time-honored celebrations and cultural observations of African Ameri-cans are quite similar in intent as for other ethnic, religious, and social groups in the U.S. — to conserve and place val-ue on the important values and legacy of one's own particular ethnic group.

1. Martin Luther King, Jr., was born January 15, 1929, in Atlanta, Georgia, where his mother and father were influential persons in the African American community.

   His mother was a schoolteacher and his father, the Reverend Martin Luther King, Sr., was a prominent second-generation Baptist minister. He was the senior minister at Ebenezar Baptist Church in Atlanta.

   By all accounts Martin, Jr., grew up in a very stable and nurturing home and community environment. One can assume that ministers, teachers, and other influential leaders in his community were persons who were dedicated to improve their communities and serve as positive role models for the young.

2. In 1517, in Wittenberg, northern Germany, an ordained priest and theologian of the Roman Catholic Church named Martin Luther, began to publicly protest some of the practices of the Church, particularly the sale of "indulgences."

Eventually, he broke ties with the Roman Catholic Church and founded a reform church body that became known as the Lutheran Church.

He and his followers stressed belief in the "priesthood of all believers," and that the Bible itself was the only authority for religious faith.

Luther became known as the great "Reformer" of the church, particularly in the eyes of those who eventually became known as "Protestant" Christians. They agreed with his stand against the Catholic Church's claim that it was the sole authority in religious matters.

In Protestant Christian history, Luther is now considered one the highest role models for leadership and dedication to one's religious conscience, even in the face of great odds.

Therefore, it must be assumed that the name "Martin Luther" had profound meaning for King Sr. and his son, Martin Jr.

3. He didn't have to take classes in the ninth and twelfth grades because of his excellent scholastic ability and intellect, and therefore graduated from Booker T. Washington High School in Atlanta at the age of 15.

   He then enrolled in his father's alma mater, Morehouse College, and at age 19, he graduated with honors, earning a Bachelor of Arts degree in Sociology in four years.

4. Following in the footsteps of his father and grandfather, Martin Jr. chose the Christian ministry as his career, and in pursuit of this goal he applied to Crozer Theological Seminary, an American Baptist graduate school located in Chester, Pennsylvania.

   He was accepted and received a scholarship to attend, and was one of the first African American students to enroll.

   In 1951, after three years of graduate study, he earned the Bachelor of Divinity degree, and in his senior year he was chosen senior class president and valedictorian.

   However, while at Crozer he was once faced with a life-threatening event when a white student from North Carolina assaulted him. The situation was peacefully resolved, mainly by King's expressed attitude to forgive the student.

In 1955, after he graduated from Crozer, Martin received an academic fellowship to cover the cost of his graduate residential Ph.D. studies at Boston University.

At B.U. he came under influence of Dr. Howard Thurman, dean of the university's chapel and a noted Christian theologian. Thurman's ideas about the oneness of the human community and integration in America apparently had a significant influence on King's philosophical views and actions.

5. Coretta Scott, who was a graduate student at Boston's New England's Conservatory of Music studying voice. She earned her undergraduate degree from Antioch College in Ohio.

In 1953, Coretta and Martin were married in Marion, Alabama, about eighty miles from Montgomery. Martin's father married them at Coretta's parents' home in the presence of many well-wishers and family members.

6. Dexter Avenue Baptist Church in Montgomery, Alabama, located near the downtown area and just several blocks south and down the hill from the Alabama State Capitol and other state buildings.

    Rev. Vernon Johns was the senior minister who preceded Dr. King at Dexter Avenue Baptist Church. He had been very active in openly challenging racial segregation and discrimination in Montgomery long before King, along with other members of the church.

7. E.D. Dixon, an influential local NAACP leader, had done a great deal to prepare the way for King's involvement in Montgomery civil rights issues.

    Likewise, the Women's Political Council in Montgomery, led by Mary Fair Burks and Jo Ann Robinson, were especially instrumental in building a consensus in the African American community to support the bus boycott in Montgomery, in an effort to end discrimination and segregation in the Montgomery bus transportation system.

8. First of all, Dr. Martin Luther King, Jr., as a Christian minister, firmly believed that racism was immoral and unjust according to his understanding of Christianity and the ideals of the American Constitution.

Secondly, he believed that he should teach and practice pacifism, and use the principle of respectful and peaceful negotiation when resolving differences between people, opposing groups, and nations.

Also, he had read and learned first-hand something about Mohandas Gandhi's philosophy and tactics of non-violence that helped India gain its freedom from England's colonialism, and become an independent nation in 1947.

In 1959, prior to his full involvement in the civil rights movement, he and his wife traveled to India in order to learn first-hand about Mohandas Gandhi's philosophy and non-violence techniques.

They learned that Gandhi's idea of non-violence was based on the Hindu religious concept of "truth force" (*satyagraha*). It is believed to be a universal spiritual principle or force that has the power to ultimately change for the better the hearts and minds of those who oppress you, and even those who hate you and would harm you in some way.

King also believed that by using both Christian

and Hindu principles of non-violence he could help bring about positive social change and justice for African Americans in the U.S.

While a student he had also read and written about Henry David Thoreau's "Civil Disobedience," a philosophical writing of the mid-1840s, which urged Americans not to pay taxes to support the U.S. war against Mexico and to take a stand against slavery.

9. In 1964, Martin Luther King, Jr., was awarded the Nobel Peace Prize in Norway for his philosophy of nonviolence and the exemplary leadership he demonstrated during the American civil rights movement of the mid-1950s into the '60s.

At age 35 he was the youngest person ever to be awarded the Nobel Peace Prize, and the second African American to receive the award. Dr. Ralph Bunche who had been an under secretary with the United Nations received the award in 1951.

Dr. King did not keep the $40,000 prize money for himself, but instead donated it to various African American non-profit organizations and humanitarian causes.

10. In April of 1963, while in a Birmingham, Alabama jail, Dr. Martin L. King, Jr., wrote his famous and profound, "Letter From a Birmingham Jail," in which he explains his views of nonviolent civil disobedience from a Christian moral perspective.

In the same context he also discusses the issue of unjust and just laws within the context of American society. Many consider his letter a classic literary masterpiece because of its objective and persuasive argument articulating American ideals.

Today, many Americans consider Dr. Martin L. King, Jr.'s, civil rights leadership, dedicated life, and death as fundamentally crucial in helping America redeem its long-tarnished spiritual soul, and to reaffirm its basic ideals of "freedom, justice and the pursuit of happiness" for all Americans.

He expressed the "Oneness" of all Americans in the following quote: "We are caught in an inescapable network of mutuality, tied in a single garment of destiny. Whatever affects one directly, affects all indirectly."

No other 20th-century American has had such a positive effect on the moral conscience of many people in the U.S. and the world.

QUIZ 29 ANSWERS
A Brief Profile of Malcolm X

1. On May 19, 1925, Malcolm X was born in Omaha, Nebraska, and given the birth name Malcolm Little.

    According to various accounts, his family was extremely dysfunctional, and he grew up in a very harsh, punitive, and unstable home and community environment.

2. At age six, after some white racists murdered his father, leaving his mother and his seven brothers and sisters to fend for themselves, Malcolm's mother suffered a serious emotional breakdown and was put in a mental institution. Malcolm and his siblings were placed in various foster homes in different cities and states.

3. In 1946, he was sentenced to ten years at the state prison at Charlestown, Massachusetts, for burglary, and while in prison, it was due to his own thirst for knowledge that he became a highly self-educated intelligent person through intensive reading and study.

    At the same time he became an ardent student of the Nation of Islam's Muslim teachings.

4. His younger brother, Reginald, introduced Malcolm to the Nation of Islam and the teachings of Elijah Muhammad, the organization's leader.

Elijah became so impressed with Malcolm's potential to become an exceptional Muslim leader that, when Malcolm was released from prison, he was mentored to become a Nation of Islam minister under Elijah.

5. When Malcolm was an assistant minister at the Nation of Islam mosque in Detroit, Michigan, he dropped "Little" as his last name, and began to use "X" instead.

He reasoned, as a number of others did, that African American last names (surnames) were essentially names arbitrarily given to freed slaves when slavery was abolished, and therefore they had no true historical value or cultural meaning related to African heritage.

6. In 1958, Malcolm X married Betty Sanders in Lansing, Michigan. She took the name, Hajj Bahijah Betty Shabazz. Their four daughters were named Attallah, Gamulah Lamumbah, Iiyasah, and Quibilah.

7. By 1963, Malcolm X had become one of the most powerful, articulate, and charismatic African American and Nation of Muslim leaders and influential speakers in the U.S. He founded the nationally circulated Nation of Islam newspaper, "Muhammad Speaks," and organized one of the largest NOI mosques in Harlem, New York.

8. Based on the racial theology unique to the Nation of Islam as a Muslim religious sect, Malcolm believed that the white race was an inferior racial group genetically engineered by a diabolic scientist by the name of "Yakub," who was in league with the devil.

   Hence, white people and their societies are by nature innately evil and harmful to the universe. Malcolm also believed, as Elijah Muhammad taught, that African people were the original human creation of God.

9. In 1964, Malcolm went to Mecca in Saudi Arabia to take part in the Muslim Hajj, or religious pilgrimage, that all devout Muslims are expected to observe as one of the basic pillars of their faith during one's lifetime.

   While in Mecca, Malcolm observed the genuine racial diversity among Muslims there. Differences in color, racial characteristics, ethnicity, and the nationality of those who had made the hajj didn't seem to matter to those making the pilgrimage. Malcolm later said that the kind of ethnic and racial diversity he observed and began to experience in Mecca caused him to rethink his previous ideas about race. Also, after his pilgrimage, he took the Muslim name of El-Hajj Malik El-Shabazz.

10. Malcolm X was assassinated in Harlem, N.Y., on February 21, 1965, allegedly by a group of former Muslims from New York City who were angry at him because of his break with Elijah Muhammad.

    There are other writers and investigators who have indicated that he may have been killed as the result of a government and/or gangster conspiracy.

Malcolm X was one of America's most effective and militant African American speakers and leaders particularly among "grass roots" African Americans living in urban inner-city areas during the 1960s.

His polemic speeches emboldened many African Americans, especially youth, to defy and challenge all vestiges of white racism in the U.S. by "any means" necessary, even if it meant being violent. He also advocated separatism during his early Muslim years.

Malcolm's charisma, wit, oratorical skills, and intelligence impressed many Americans, white as well as black. Nevertheless, mainstream media tended to label him a "racial agitator," whose ideas were setting back race relations in the U.S.

On the other hand, many African Americans were becoming more emboldened to assert themselves in dealing with whites generally, and to take more overt pride in their "blackness."

Perhaps his greatest legacy was to speak out clearly about the great hypocrisy in ideals

---

and practices of America when it comes to the actual rights, opportunities, and living conditions of African Americans compared to white Americans.

Also, like Martin L. King, Jr., he was committed to bringing about positive changes for African Americans, a cause for which he gave his life.

And in one of his speeches he expressed hs dream for all Americans in the following quote: "...in all honesty and sincerity it can be stated that I wish nothing but freedom, justice, equality, life, liberty and the pursuit of happiness for all people."

QUIZ 30 ANSWERS

Origin and Brief Overview of African American Muslims in the U.S.

1. These are words that have their origin in Arabic language and have the following meanings when translated into English:

   a. *Allah* = the One Supreme Being.

   b. *Islam* = obedience and/or surrender to Allah.

   c. *Muslim* = one who submits to the will of Allah.

   d. *Qur'an* = sacred book of recitations (revelations) from Allah to Muhammad, the last prophet.

   e. *Mosque* = place of prostration and worship before Allah.

   f. *Imam* = the leader of a Muslim community.

   g. *Mullah* = interpreter of teacher of Muslim sacred law.

   h. *Jihad* = the duty to excel in all things, especially in the struggle against evil, and in defending Islam.

   i. *Ummah* = Muslim congregation or community of believers.

   j. *As-Salaam alaikum* = peace be with you (and security) in Allah, and *Wa-alaikum salaam* = I return that peace. (These two greetings are universal among Muslims).

---

2. Muhammad ibn Abdullah who is considered to be the last true prophet of Allah after Abraham, Moses, and Jesus. He founded Islam in 613 C. E. when he began to publicly recite his revelations from Allah to the people. Now they are written down in the Qur'an. The Qur'an is considered to be the holy book or scriptures of Islam.

3. The Five Pillars of Islam are five religious duties required of all Muslims regardless of the particular organized sect. In numerical order they are:

a. *Shahadah*, making the basic utterance that "there is no God but Allah, and Muhammad is his prophet."

b. *Salat*, performing ritual prayer five times a day, preferably at the community mosque, and particularly for the Friday noon prayer.

c. *Sawm* or fasting, especially during Ramadan, the ninth month in the Islamic calendar, which is usually in the fall. During this time, all Muslims are to refrain from drink, food, tobacco, and sexual activity every day from dawn to dusk in order to enhance self-restraint.

d. *Zakat*, or giving of one's material wealth to help those in need, and to give to further the cause of truth through the Islamic community and not as an individual.

e. *Hajj*, or making a pilgrimage to the holy city of Mecca in Saudi Arabia during one's lifetime or having a proxy do it for you. Muslims believe that by going to this holy center of Islam they can reaffirm their faith in the unity and oneness of Allah and the Muslim religious community.

4. It is estimated that, in addition to the Nation of Islam (NOI) and the American Society of Muslims (ASM), there are at least twelve other different and autonomous African American Muslim communities in the U.S. today.

5. Wali Fard Muhammad started the NOI in Detroit, Michigan, in 1930, and Elijah Muhammad (1897-1975), who became a convert and devout aide to Fard, further developed the growth and program of the NOI when he became its leader in Chicago beginning in 1934.

   The main thrust and appeal of the Nation of Islam in the U.S. is to lead African Americans to self-reliance, self-determination, total community development and progress, and to take positive steps to eliminate racism in the U.S. wherever it exists.

   One of the attractions for some young men is the emphasis on mastery of self-defense tehniques, and a healthy and upright lifestyle.

6. Louis Farrakhan (1933-) became the "Honorable Minister" or leading Imam in the NOI shortly after the death of Elijah Muhammad in 1975. Two of his major achievements in the 1990s were organizing and leading the "Million Man March" and the "Million Family March" in Washington, D.C.

   He has also been very successful in providing well-organized leadership and direction not only for the NOI but in many respects for the broader African American community.

7. The headquarters of the Nation of Islam is in Chicago, Illinois, and it is estimated that that there are tens of thousands of members throughout the U.S..

8. After Minister Elijah Muhammad's death, his son Warith Deen Muhammad reorganized the Nation of Islam into the World Community of Islam and then into the American Society of Muslims. Today, there are more than 300 affiliated mosques in different parts of the U.S.

9. The headquarters for the American Muslim Society is also in Chicago, and there are an estimated tens of thousands of members.

---

10. a. Mohammad Ali, the world's greatest heavyweight boxing champion in the 20th century.

b. Kareem Abdul Jabar, Hall of Fame NBA basketball player.

c. Chavis Muhammad of the Nation of Islam (aka Benjamin Chavis, former Christian minister and CORE leader).

d. Hakeem Olajuwon, former NBA star with the Houston Rockets.

e. Wallace Deen Muhammad, leader of the American Muslim Society.

African American Muslims represent diverse and influential religious communities that were founded and evolved in U.S. urban inner-city areas during the 20th century. The Nation of Islam and the American Muslim Mission have the largest number of followers. However, there are other much smaller African American Muslim religious groups in such places as Buffalo, NY, and Cleveland, OH.

The growth and success of African American Muslims is their faith and commitment in meeting the educational, health, economic, socio-political, and spiritual needs of many people in urban communities.

Their religious emphasis on family, community and economic solidarity, and healthy living has resulted in recruiting many persons from the culture of mainstream American society.

Also, the successful rehabilitation and recruitment of many African American inmates in jail and prison has helped to add to their numbers.

Contrary to some media characterizations,

the leadership structure of African American Muslim religious groups is not cultic. It is part of a democratic selection process based on ability, education, seniority, moral integrity, and dedication. There are a significant number of women and professionals who are also a part of the leadership.

Unfortunately, in the aftermath of 9/11 some African American Muslims have been wrongly profiled, detained and interrogated at airports by tactless Homeland Security personnel and by various law enforcement agents, mainly because of their Arabic sounding names or style of dress.

1. In 1735, one of Europe's leading natural scientists and taxonomists, Carolus Linnaeus (1707-78), separated the human race into four distinct racial group categories or classes. He also described certain physical traits and behavior as typical characteristics for each group as follows:

   a. Africans were described as slow and not giving proper care and attention, yet cunning, prone to be capricious, and "happy-go-lucky."

   b. American Indians as obstinate, yet free and easily contented.

   c. Asiatic or Asians as very proud, with strong opinions and quite harsh in manner.

   d. Europeans as very intelligent, creative, and superior to the other groups.

   Linnaeus' "hierarchy of races" theory soon became the basis for most European definitions of race for many centuries, and it wasn't until the late 20th century that modern scientists refuted his theory. Nevertheless, the legacy of his unscientific thinking about race is still believed by some people today.

2. "Race" is a term that is commonly used to refer to a person or group of people whose obvious external or extrinsic physical traits, such as skin color, hair texture, and eye shape distinguish them from other racial groups.

   However, between 1950 and 1968, many world-renowned scientists concluded that such traits do not definitively indicate a person's racial ancestry, but that such intrinsic traits as DNA and blood type are more accurate indicators of racial ancestry.

   They also concluded that there is only one race – the human race – and that there are no separate or pure races among humans.

3. Nowhere in the Bible is there any clearly stated references to "race" or "racial group" differences associated with the skin color of any of the different ethnic and religious groups mentioned.

   The only exception is the Queen of Sheba. She refers to herself as "I am black, but comely," or Black and good-looking as described in the Bible (Song of Solomon 1:5).

4. The majority of today's scientists take the position that even though some 20th-century I.Q. test score differences seemed to exist between some "racial" groups, there is no scientific evidence that any one group has innate intellectual superiority over another.

   When there are such differences, the evidence indicates that it is related more to educational, language, cultural, and environmental differences that can either enhance or limit intellectual ability and performance.

5. Melanin is the name of the chemical substance or granules that give color or pigment to the skin, hair, and eyes of human beings. The amount and type of color in these external parts of the body basically depends on an individual's genetic ancestry, and the geographical environment where one lives.

Persons who have dark-skinned African ancestors and who have not interbred with light-skinned Europeans will most likely have complexions similar to their African ancestors. But even within this ancestral pool there are different gradations of skin color.

Individuals who do not have any skin melanin in their bodies are referred to genetically as "albinos" and represent a very small percentage of the human population; they are found among African, Asian, and European populations.

Melanin in human skin helps to filter the sun's ultraviolet rays and protect the skin from being burned from sun exposure. It is also related to some other biological and chemical processes in the body, especially those involved in the production of Vitamin D and calcium in the body.

6. The Nazi "Aryan Race" theory is based in part on the philosophical racial thinking of Comte Joseph Arthur de Gobineau, a 19th-century French writer. In the

mid-1850s he wrote an essay entitled the "Inequality of Human Races," in which he reasoned that there was a hierarchy of races similar to Linnaeus' theory.

He further claimed that within the European race itself there was a superior "Aryan" level or racial segment that was inherently destined to rule and take care of the classes below them.

This idea became the basis for *noblesse oblige* thinking – the notion that the ruling classes of Europe were destined and obliged to take care of the masses of people.

Such thinking also became an important rationalization as well as justification for much of European colonization in Africa, Asia, and the New World for many centuries.

Adolph Hitler and the Nazis also adopted this kind of racial thinking. They further interpreted it to support their own notions of racial superiority, and the necessity for ethnic cleansing and the extermination of Jewish people.

Hitler's autobiographical book, "Mein Kampf (My Struggle)," described his racial ideas and his hatred of Jews, a book which became a primary basis for Nazi Germany's extermination of an estimated twelve million Jews and other ethnic minority groups in Europe during World War II.

7. Racial hybridization refers to ethnic/racial group interbreeding ("racial mixing"), especially when a person of one genetically different racial background interbreeds with a person of a different racial background.

Currently, in the U.S. as well as in some European countries and other parts of the world, racial hybridization is quite observable and is becoming more prevalent, acceptable, and appreciated than ever before.

Much of the racial hybridization that has taken place in the U.S. between persons of European and African racial background took place during the many centuries of African enslavement when European men impregnated African slave women with impunity.

Hence, today this is reflected in the multiple-complexions, different hair colors, and other physical characteristics found among the African American population.

In the past, the die-hard racist has referred to racial hybridization by using such demeaning terms as "mongrelization," "half-breed" and "half-caste," for the purpose of stereotyping an individual or a group as being inferior and not "racially pure." Racial hybridization has been a reality for humans to a greater or lesser extent throughout history.

8. Depending on the particular athletic or sports activities, persons from each of these groups have demonstrated superior abilities for which they trained and were motivated to succeed at doing.

In recent years a considerable number of African Americans and other ethnic minority groups have excelled in a diversity of sports such as tennis, golf and ice-skating; sports that were considered to be "white."

They have excelled mainly because of their own ability, desire to win, and the equal opportunity afforded to them to compete, not because of their ethnic and racial group ancestry.

9. Depending upon where such studies are made (regional, urban, or suburban locations), it is estimated that anywhere from 20 to 75 percent of African Americans are genetically or racially mixed with European ancestors and Native American ancestors.

A close observation of a cross-section of the African American population will reflect varying degrees of genetic racial mixing.

10. One of the most pervasive and egregious myths projected about African Americans is that by nature they are more sexually active and virile than other groups of people.

Much of this notion in American culture has to do with past stereotypical perceptions of male and female sexuality among slaves and between some men and women in certain urban "ghettos."

Likewise, some have perceived what seems to be less inhibited expressions of sexuality among some African Americans in such contexts as dance, song, comedy, and language, and have concluded that this means that the entire group has an abnormally heightened interest in sex.

Certain movies, television and radio programs, and other media have greatly reinforced negative stereotypes about African American sexuality as well as other expressions of behavior.

It is interesting to note that there are similar kinds of stereotypes that are still expressed about the heightened sexuality of the so-called "Latins:" the French, Spanish and Italians.

"Scientists have reached general agreement in recognizing that mankind is one: that all men (and women) belong to the same species., Homo sapiens. *It is further generally agreed among scientists that all men are probably derived from the same common stock; and that such differences as exist between different groups of mankind are due to the operation of evolutionary factors of differentiation such as isolation, the drift and random fixation of the material particles which control heredity (the genes), changes in the structure of these particles, hybridization, and natural selection."*

—Ashley Montagu, "Statement on Race"

A more recent declaration of the Convention on the Elimination of Racial Discrimintion states, "…any doctrine of superiority based on racial differentiation is scientifically false, morally condemnable, socially unjust and dangerous…"

QUIZ 32 ANSWERS

Unforgettable Flagrant Acts of Brutality, Dehumanization, Disfranchisement & Terrorism Suffered by African Americans

1. Slaves were branded on their buttocks, and some women on their breasts. Also, some had their ear lobes clipped and were forced to wear a neck brace and leg irons, especially during the period of their initial captivity.

2. Runaway slaves had certain toes or fingers removed, and in some horrendous cases had a foot or leg amputated.

   A whip was used to severely lash or beat a disobedient slave (male or female), and was the usual means of punishment. This was often done in public at a "whipping post," to demonstrate to other slaves what would happen to an unruly slave, and sexual assaults against recalcitrant slave women were not uncommon and carried out for the same purpose.

3. Plantation owners often hired an "overseer," usually a white male, to manage the overall operations of a plantation.

Supervising and working with the slave "driver," or a labor foreman, he would determine what work was to be done, and how to get maximum effort out of the slaves.

A driver was usually a poor white male, but in a few cases a trusted slave would be given this responsibility.

A driver used both punitive and reward methods in order to get the slaves to perform their tasks either as individuals or in groups. It might mean giving them more rest time, food and water, or some other tangible reward.

On the other hand, if the overseer or driver thought that the work wasn't done according to the goals set, it could result in slaves receiving fewer benefits, and ultimately being whipped as punishment.

4. In the last year of the Civil War, when more than 300 Union Army Colored Troopers, and some women and children, were captured by Confederate Army forces, they were subsequently massacred.

   Gen. Nathan Forrest, their infamous commander, would not accept their surrender, and instead ordered his men to shoot and torch the soldiers and civilians without mercy. This murderous act on the part of the Confederate soldiers goes down in history as the worst atrocity of the Civil War.

5. In 1865, in the same year that the 13th Amendment was passed by Congress to abolish slavery throughout the U.S., the Ku Klux Klan (KKK) was organized in Pulaski, Tennessee, by former Confederate Army officer Nathan Forrest.

   He and those who founded the group stated that their purpose was to preserve white Christian (Protestant) civilization.

   The use of Greek language terms, wearing of white robes, and burning crosses became effective symbols, communicating the clandestine and secret nature of the terrorist organization.

   The real purpose and intent of the KKK was to intimidate and prevent African Americans from exercising their full citizenship rights, and to reassert southern white supremacy by any means necessary.

The Klan used such techniques as tarring and feathering its victims, setting fire to their houses, churches, and farm buildings, and destroying their crops and livestock.

The KKK was also usually the perpetrator of widespread lynchings in the South, and the outright murder of individuals, both white and black, whom they felt opposed their agenda.

Even though Congress passed laws to curtail the unlawful and terrorist activities of the KKK in 1870-71, by 1926 the Klan had a national membership of nearly nine million when it boldly paraded down Pennsylvania Avenue in Washington, D.C.

By this time the KKK was also targeting and attacking Catholics, Jewish Americans, Chinese, and Mexican immigrants as its enemies.

6. *Plessy* v. *Ferguson.* This U.S. Supreme Court case decision in 1896 gave the right to legally discriminate and segregate "Negroes" from whites in public accomodations.

Separate seating arrangements on trains, separate schools, separate drinking fountains, and separate restrooms, etc., were permitted so long as they were "equal."

Such "Jim Crow" laws were usually enforced and not interpreted as unconstitutional until the 1954 *Brown* v. *Topeka* Supreme Court decision which overturned the 1896 decision of the Court.

7. a. In September, 1906, in an all-out effort to intimidate and prevent African American voters in Atlanta, Georgia, from voting, white mobs attacked and severely beat them during several days of rioting. Both whites and Blacks were killed, and as a result very few African American citizens voted.

b. In July of 1917, one of the nation's worst race riots in the north took place in East St.Louis, Illinois. Unruly white mobs attacked and killed forty African Americans in their own communities. In some cases they set their homes on fire, and when some of them tried to escape from the terror they were shot. The underlying issue was resentment against African

Americans who were moving into white housing areas, and who were portrayed and perceived as a threat to white jobs and social status.

"The Josephine Baker Story" movie, starring Lynn Whitfield, dramatizes this historical event.

c. For two days, May 31-June 1, 1921, in Tulsa, Oklahoma, one of the most prosperous well-established African American communities in the state and the nation became a domestic war zone.

Thousands of white militant, vigilante-type white Tulsans went on a rampage. They used clubs, torches, rifles, and even machine guns to attack and kill an estimated 150-200 of the town's African American citizens, and scores of whites were also killed. Block after block of African American homes and businesses were set fire, as well as some churches.

The issue that provoked the carnage and destruction was a rumor that a black youth had raped a white girl, an allegation that was later found to be untrue.

d. In 1998, three self-proclaimed white supremacists kidnapped James Byrd, Jr., an African American, beat him, chained him to the back of their truck by his ankles and dragged him on a country road for more than two miles until he died.

Two of these supremacists received the death penalty, and the third one was sentenced to life in prison.

8. a. In the summer of 1955, while visiting in Mississippi, 14-year-old Emmett Till was brutally beaten to death by two white men who tied his body to an anchor and then submerged it in a nearby river.

Till had been accused of wrongly speaking to a local white woman. Although Roy Bryant and J.W. Milam were arrested and charged with the crime, both were acquitted by an all-white jury.

b. Without any provocation, on Jun13, 1963, Byron De La Beckwith used a rifle to shoot and kill Medgar Evers, an NAACP field secretary, while Evers was standing in the driveway of his home.

Even though Beckwith was tried twice for killing Evers, Mississippi justice did not convict him until 1994, more than 60 years later.

c. In August of 1964 the battered and drowned bodies of James Chaney, Andrew Goodman, and Michael Schwerner were found near an earth-made river dam in Philadelphia, Mississippi. Chaney (21), a young African American from Mississippi, was traveling by car with Goodman (20) and Schwerner (24), two young white men from New York.

They were working with CORE and other civil rights groups in an effort to register African American voters in the area.

It wasn't until June, 2005, that 80-year-old Edgar

Ray Killen was convicted of manslaughter for the killing of the three civil rights workers.

9.   On a quiet Sunday morning on September 15, 1963, one of the most heinous tragedies ever to take place in the nation's history occurred in Birmingham, Alabama.

Four African American youths attending Sunday school classes, one who was 11 years old and three who were 14 years old, were killed by a bomb explosion outside the Sixteenth Street Baptist Church they were attending. Twenty others were also injured.

Many Americans in all parts of the country were horrified and outraged at the time, and wanted those responsible brought to justice.

Eventually, four members of the Ku Klux Klan were arrested and charged with the crime, but were never convicted and brought to justice until the late 1970s.

It wasn't until May, 2002, that the only living remaining of member of the four original Klansmen, Bobby F. Cherry, 71 years old, was tried and finally convicted of the children's murder and sent to prison. He had escaped earlier conviction by being ruled incompetent.

10. After completing the required Reserve Officer training program at Fort Benning, Georgia, Lt. Col. Penn, while driving his car, was viciously shot pointblank with a shotgun by two members of the Athens, Georgia, Ku Klux Klan, who drove up alongside of him, shot, and murdered him. They were eventually convicted and sentenced to ten years in prison.

EBONY OWL: DID YOU KNOW?

No other minority population group indigenous to the U.S. (racial, ethnic, religious or otherwise) has been brutalized, oppressed, and victimized by terrorism and injustice as much as African Americans.

Also, no other group of Americans has been systematically denied their fundamental human and Constitutional rights for so many centuries because of color and race as have African Americans.

Any future material and moral reparations that are justly owed to African Americans can only partially provide for the full restitution of the centuries of personal and group suffering endured by this group of Americans.

The current wave of global terrorism by which

many are being victimized and tragically harmed is but a solemn reminder to many African Americans of the centuries of terrorism that they and their ancestors have experienced in the U.S.

Hopefully, 21st-century America will become a safe, equitable and righteous place for all of its citizens regardless of race, creed or color.

QUIZ 33 ANSWERS
Exceptional 20th Century Giants for Equal Rights and Justice in the U.S

1. Adam Clayton Powell, Sr., (1865-1953) and Adam Clayton Powell, Jr., (1908-1972) of Harlem's Abyssinian Baptist Church, which is still one of the largest African American churches in the U.S..

2. Charles H. Houston (1885-1950).

3. Constance B. Motley (1921-).

4. Dorothy I. Height (1912-).

5. Marion W. Edelman (1939-).

6. Fannie Lou Hamer (1917-1977).

7. Jesse L. Jackson (1941-).

8. Daisy Bates (1922-).

9. Angela Davis (1944-).

10.   William B. Rumford, Sr. (1908-1986).

EBONY OWL: DID YOU KNOW?

Although he was overshadowed by Thurgood Marshall and psychologist Dr. Kenneth Clark in the Brown v. Topeka *U.S. Supreme Court proceedings, another NAACP attorney also played an important role.*

Robert L. Carter took a lead role in the case because he actually organized the NAACP's judicial plan of argument to present to the Court.

Carter himself had to overcome an economically impovershed background, but through hard work and determination eventually completed his law studies at Howard and Columbia universities, and afterwards was employed by the NAACP.

1. Phillis Wheatley and Susannah and John Wheatley.

2. Prudence Crandall.

3. John Quincy Adams, 6th U.S. President (1825-29).

4. Thaddeus Stevens and Charles Sumner.

5. Mrs. Eleanor Roosevelt, Marian Anderson, and Franklin D. Roosevelt, 32nd U.S. President (1933-45).

6. Jack London and Jenny Prentiss. "Call of the Wild," and "White Fang."

7. President Harry S. Truman, 33rd U.S. President (1945-1953).

8. President Lyndon B. Johnson, 36th U.S. President (1963-69).

9. Matthew A. Henson. It is now well known that on April 6, 1909, it was actually Hensen who was the first to reach the North Pole and plant the U.S. flag.

   Unfortunately, for many years Henson's accomplishment went unrecognized and unrewarded. It wasn't until he was more than 70-years-old that he was given credit.

   In special caremonies, both Presidents Harry S. Truman and Dwight Eisenhower honored him, and after Henson died at age 91 he was buried in Arlington National Cementary with military honors.

10. Coach John Hayden Fry, Jr., and player Jerry LeVias.

Throughout American history, from colonial times to the present, there has been a minority of white Americans who have actively taken a forthright stand to oppose racial oppression and injustice of any kind directed toward African Americans and other minority groups, and they have worked with them and for them.

In the past these courageous Americans have been labeled with derogatory names such as "social agitators," "nigger lovers," or "communists," or stereotyped with some other kind of negative image that would brand them as radicals and un-American.

Unfortunately, a biased media and narrow-minded politicians also expressed views to reinforce these stereotypes.

Yet, when we look at positive social changes in America, the fact remains that courageous persons like those mentioned above have demonstrated a moral integrity and a true American spirit that have helped the nation to live up to its highest ideals.

Now, in the 21st-century, there is a growing awareness of the first-class citizenship rights and opportunities that all Americans should have, and although not always apparent, there is an increasing number of white and other Americans who are committed and quite proactive in helping to bring this about, as are African Americans.

QUIZ 35 ANSWERS
"Black Culture" and "Ebonics": Myths and Facts

1. Beginning in the 1660s, with the arrival of the first Africans in the British colony of Virginia, to the present time, there is a clearly defined viable and meaningful African American culture in the U.S.

   It is expressed through a diversity of institutions, program activities, shared beliefs, and values, and a distinctive ethnic minority group identity.

   It is a culture that is basically American grown, but one that is a synthesis of the dominant Anglo-American culture and some aspects of African culture.

   Similar to other ethnic groups that make up the U.S. population such as Irish American, Jewish American, Chinese American, Mexican American, or others, African Americans are just one ethnic group in the total of American society that has its own distinctive history and culture.

2. Historically, the first source of African American culture came from the African slaves and the various tribal cultures from which they came. They brought their own ideals, beliefs, languages, and practices about the nature, meaning, and purpose of life.

As slaves they were coerced to give up their African tribal cultures and were compelled to take on limited aspects of Anglo-American culture. Eventually, a unique African American slave culture took root that grew and was passed on for many generations.

Although slave culture reflected the oppressive slave living and working conditions, and demeaning master-slave interpersonal relationships, there were some positive characteristics. For example, the slave family placed positive value on monogamy, parental responsibility and kinship networks.

Slave culture also shaped a certain pattern of male-female relationships, family structure, life style, and the development of self and group concept, some of it positive as well as negative according to some scholars.

In a very basic and therapeutic way, when most slaves and their descendents became converts to Christianity, the Christian religion became a primary and powerful spiritual resource for them.

It enabled them to persevere in the most inhumane circumstances, and brought comfort in believing there would be a better life in the future.

It also inspired and empowered others to resist the evils of slavery and racial oppression, and to strive for better times in the future.

3. a. Hollywood and television images of celebrities in the entertainment and sports arenas.

    b. Instant material gratification.

    c. Easy, mellow, and recreational life style.

    d. Emphasis on sexual freedom and promiscuous relationships.

    e. Use of both legal and illegal drugs to relieve stressful situations, as well as to get a "high."

4. a. Religious faith and orientation toward a belief in God.

    b. Acqiring an education, skills, and going to college.

    c. Family solidarity and kinship loyalty.

    d. Moral integrity in personal and interpersonal relations.

    e. Racial pride and respect for elders.

5. Religious institutions, the family, educational institutions, economic institutions, historical societies, museums, literary and artistic institutions, civil rights organizations, sororities and fraternities, as well as other social institutions, and many others too numerous to list in this book.

Also, since the 1970s, there has been a tremendous growth in well-established African American historical and cultural museums and libraries throughout the U.S. In many ways they are collectively becoming one of the greatest repositories of African American history and culture under the control and direction of African Americans themselves.

6. The terms "Black Language," "Black English," and "Ebonics" all refer to a dialect of standard or formal American English that is spoken by some African Americans in certain language and communication settings.

Most African Americans, however, speak a conversational form of standard American English as their primary first language, and so-called Black English usually functions like a second language for those who speak it.

However, for a considerable number of African Americans who grow up in a predominantly Black English or Ebonics language dialect environment, this may be their first and primary language of communication and meaning.

However, usually when they go to school and are formally taught standard English for at least twelve years, Black English becomes the secondary English language dialect, and many may become as proficient in standard English usage as any other American.

The vast majority of African Americans speak standard English and on the whole have never been highly motivated, or see any practical value, to study and learn an African language. This was the case for a small minority in the latter decades of the 20th century when there was considerable emphasis on learning and appreciating one's African culture roots.

7. a. "Black Power" and "Black is Beautiful" are phrases that were quite often expressed by African Americans during the 1960s-70s. The term Black Power placed emphasis on group solidarity and unity, especially with respect to using political power and various kinds of activism to bring about social justice and equality of economic, educational, and political opportunity.
b. "Black is Beautiful" is a phrase that places emphasis on the notion that the color "black" is beautiful, and that contrary to the many English language synonyms that essentially refer to it as something which is dirty, dismal, sullen, and even demonic in some way, the term Black is Beautiful perceives the physical color of African Americans and any other of their physical traits as beautiful.

The use of the word "black" in each of these expressions was very effective in redefining the word to have positive meaning and value rather than have negative conotations. For several decades the positive use of the word "black" and the expression "Black is Beautiful" have greatly helped to enhance the self-concept and group concept of many African Americans. Also, the renewed emphasis placed on taking pride in the contributions of African civilization to human civilization, and the various contributions of African Americans to America reinforced the positive meaning of these words.

Nevertheless, there were and are still some who perceive the use of these terms as racist, agitative, and even divisive.

The raised arm with the clenched fist demonstratd by medalist Tommy Smith and John Carlos at the 1968 Olympics symbolized "Black Power," and wearing the Afro hairstyle and African clothing styles similar to the *dashiki* was for the purpose of identifying with one's ethnic group.

It was not to symbolize racial superiority. Also, many African American youth at this time began to wear black leather jackets and berets to associate themselves with members of the Black Panther Party.

In some instances, these non-verbal symbols of "blackness" were perceived to be extremely radical, intimidating, and even consideered un-American.

Today, however, the term "African American" has become the more widely used and acceptable positive group reference term, because it links African historical and cultural roots with meaningful American heritage. This seems to be the sentiment of most African Americans even though they cannot trace their ancestral roots to any particular tribe, place, or person in Africa.

8. The following ten words and terms are African or African American in origin and are used every day more or less by most Americans:
   a. banana
   b. banjo
   c. "right on!"
   d. gig
   e. gumbo
   f. jazz
   g. junkie
   h. okay
   i. tote
   j. yam

9. "Moms" Mabley (Loretta Mary Aiken) and Redd Foxx, Dick Gregory and Richard Pryor.

10. "Soul" refers to the perceived spiritual part of African American personality and culture that ideally expresses itself through deep feelings of belonging, togetherness and shared experience.

   African Americans believe it to be an attribute common to themselves because of a common heritage related to enslavement of ancestors, oppressive racism, perseverance to survive, and the righteous struggle for change in the present and future.

At the beginning of the 21st century it seems quite evident that African American culture and society is a reality that co-exists with and is integral to the larger context of American culture and society, and that both are being mutually influenced and changed in a number of significant ways.

One of the most obvious examples of this is to be found in the increasing number of established museums and libraries that exist at the local, regional, and national levels throughout the U.S., some that focus on various aspects of African American life and experience, and others that are valuable repositories of information about this group of Americans.

It also seems reasonable to predict that as institutional racism is effectively eliminated in the U.S., and successive generations of African Americans increasingly internalize American middle class core values and are provided with equal opportunities enabling them to take on various roles and responsibilities in society, they will more and more be perceived as Americans, persons who just happen to have African American ancestry.

This does not mean, however, that African Americans will automatically abandon their own ethnic culture and institutions. This heritage continues to be extremely valuable for African Americans, individually and collectively, and this fact should not be interpreted in any way that African Americans devalue the positive parts of their American heritage, nor that they are unpatriotic. Rather it should be seen as an American made ethnic/racial group taking pride in its successful struggle for shaping American ideals and practices of freedom and justice, and helping to make their nation the best that it is today.

Furthermore, if future white American interaction and relations with African Americans are ones of mutual respect, cooperation, and friendly relations, it might also result in the dominant white society doing more to assimilate and adopt certain aspects of African American culture.

1. The word "Rap" refers to a genre or type of music that basically combines the use of song lyrics and music in a syncopated manner, and often in a repetitive manner.

   One of the key persons in expressing this kind of music is the disc jockey (DJ), who in an artistic and stylistic way uses such techniques as "scratching" and "mixing" the recordings that are being played for the purpose of evoking a certain kind of response from those at a dance, block or street party, or concert.

   The DJ and/or main performer(s) also use a microphone to "rap" with the music in such a way as to evoke responses from the listener.

   The song lyrics in Rap music are varied but are basically words designed to express certain ideas, feelings and attitude. Some lyrics are considered to be quite harmful, unconventional and counter to mainstream culture (e.g. "gangsta" and sexist Rap).

   On the other hand some Rap music is thought to be positive and constructive (e.g. "Christian" and "kid" Rap).

   "Hip-Hop" is a term that refers to the evolution of

original Rap music into a much larger cultural form or institution. It now includes many types and techniques of Rap music, but also involves various kinds of break dancing routines, dress and clothing styles, graffiti art, and billions of dollars of commercialization.

2. Rap music began in the U.S. in the early 1970s through the initial efforts of disk jockey Kook Herc in New York, and other DJs like Grandmaster Flash, Afrika Bambaataa, and Grand Wizard, whose techniques in playing records with "breaks" in the flow of music, and "scratching," attracted the attention and following of many youth.

3. "M.C. Hammer" became the stage name of Stanley Burrell, who introduced his animated spectacular break dancing routine with Rap music in 1979. "M.C." stands for master of ceremonies.

4. "Rapper's Delight": "I said a hip-hop the hippie the hippi to the hip hip hop, a you don't stop' the rock it to the bang bang boogie say up jumped the boogie to the rhythm of the boogie, the beat to, the beat."

5. Russell Simmons, who founded Def Jam Records with Rick Rubin in 1984, is now considered the "Grandfather" of Hip-Hop mainly because of his successful efforts to help lay the foundation for a billion dollar Hip-Hop economy in the U.S. and eventually in other countries such as Germany and Japan.

6. It was Def Jam Records that launched rapper LL Cool J. ("ladies love cool James) into becoming an award-winner actor and rapper.
   a. In 1990, the hit movie "Boyz N the Hood" stars Ice Cube, who goes on to have major roles in other movies.
   b. LL Cool J. (Ladies love cool James).
   c. Snoop Doggy Dogg, who recently teamed up with retired CEO Lee Iacocca of Chrysler to rap in their 2005 car ads.
   d. The all-around Hip-Hop entertainment entrepreneur, Sean "P. Diddy" Combs, has become a very important role model and influential person for many urban youth as well as a creative sponsor for Hip Hop artists and music. His successful efforts to overcome deficiencies in his early education are much to be admired.

7. Queen Latifah (born Dana Evans) was nominated for an Oscar for her superb acting role as "Mama Morton" in the movie "Chicago" and recently starred in the movie "Beauty Shop."

8. Debbie Harry and Eminem.

9. Tupac Shakur was killed in a drive-by shooting in Las Vegas in 1996, and "Notorious B.I.G." (Biggy Smalls) was also killed by gunfire in Los Angeles the following year.

   Some have rumored that the deaths of the two men were related to a bitter conflict between the two Rappers and competition between their supporters.

10. a. bling-bling = bright and shiny jewelry.
    b. cabbage patch = a slow rhythmic one-person dance often appearing in Kentucky Fried Chicken television ads picturing an animated and happy Colonel Sanders.
    c. dis = reject, demean, ignore, criticize or put down someone.
    d. Djing = musically and artistically mixing the right music or instrument to a rapper's voice.
    e. hizzle = outrageous, unbelievable, even wild.
    f. playa hata = someone who resents other people for having more than they.

g. shorty = a woman.

h. street cred = a person with a reputation as a thug.

i. tizzle = emotionally disturbed or upset.

j. wack = something that is clearly wrong or inappropriate.

Some Hip-Hop historians trace the roots of Rap and Hip-Hop back to African culture and music, and also to African American slave culture and to the further development of African American genres of music, as expressed in both worship and entertainment.

However, today, Hip-Hop is firmly entrenched in many segments of American culture and its origin in the U.S. began in the urban streets and environments of African American inner-city New York.

It can no longer be thought of as exclusively African American. It is expressed in many places throughout the U.S., and is now found in many countries throughout the world. It is a 21st-century music and entertainment phenomena.

Although the above paragraphs are basically a descriptive analysis of the development of rap, it must be said that the musical lyrics and dance of much of today's Hip-Hop in the U.S. unfortunately reflects a degrading stereotype of African American women's sexual identity. There is also a serious concern on the part of some that the degrading type of Hip-Hop undermines conventional African American standards of morality and decent behavior. It is the view of a number of reputable and well-meaning persons that much more has to be done to clean up the "bad" Hip-Hop and emphasize more positive Hip-Hop. The challenge is to those who create and promote Hip-Hop, and to those who consume it.

1. The total population of African Americans in the 2000 census was reported to be 36,419,434, or 12.9 % of the total U.S. population of 281,421,906. The Hispanic population of 35,305,818 is the largest minority population, with 12.5% of the total U.S. population.

2. New York (3,014,385), Texas (2,404,566), Georgia (2,349,542), Florida (2,335,505), and California (2,263,882).

3. New York City (2,129,762), Chicago (1,065,009), Detroit (775,772), Philadelphia (655,824), Houston (494,496).

4. Mississippi total of 2,573,216 with AA total of 1,033,809 or 36.3%.

   Louisiana total of 4,219,973 with AA total of 1,451,944 or 32.5%.

   South Carolina total of 3,486,703 with AA total of 1,185,216 or 29.5%.

   Georgia total of 6,478,216 with AA total of 2,349,542 or 28.7%.

   Maryland total of 4,781,468 with AA total of 1,477,411 or 27.9%.

5. Married couples 819,000 or 36.79%; divorced 2,765,000 or 11.5%; widowed 1,692,000 or 7.0%.

6. 363,000.

7. According to 2002 U.S. Census data, nearly 50% of all African American family households were maintained by married couples, 43.4% by single mothers, and 8.7% by single fathers.

8. a. According to 2000 census data, the educational attainment of some 20 million African Americans, ages 25 and over, is 78.5% with 4 years high school or more, 43.3% with some college or more, and 16.5% 4 years with college or more.

   b. In 2000, according to the U.S. Department of Justice, 56.8% (791,6000) of African American men over the age of 17 were in prison. This compares to 603,032 enrolled in college. This figure has risen over 5 times since 1980 when there were 143,000 Black men in prison and 463,700 in college.

9. It was $31,778 according to 2000 Census data, and in 2002 there was an increase to $33,598, but less than the $55,000 median for white Americans in 2000.

10. In 2002, 65.8% of African American or 15,334,000 were employed in the civilian work force compared to 67.4% for white Americans or 113,475,000. In 2003, 11.8 of African Americans were unemployed compared to 5.5% for whites.

Ever since U.S. Census statistics have been kept about the poverty in the U.S., African Americans as a group have always had the highest numbers of persons living at the poverty level.

Recent 2004 U.S. Census Bureau figures indicate that African Americans represent 24.7% of the total 37 million persons living at the poverty level in the U.S.

In 2003, a family of four having an income of $19,307 or less, and family of two at $12,334, were considered living in poverty. The median household income in 2003 was $44,389.

EPILOGUE OF QUOTES

THE AMERICAN'S CREED

"I believe in the United States of America as a government
of the people, for the people; whose just powers are derived from the consent of the governed; a democracy in
a republic; a sovereign Nation of many sovereign States;
a perfect union, one and inseparable; established upon
those principles of freedom, equality, justice, and humanity for which American patriots sacrificed their
lives and fortunes.

I therefore believe it is my duty to my country to love it, to
support its Constitution, to obey its laws, to respect its
flag, and to defend it against all enemies."

—William Tyler Page, 1917

AMERICA, THE BEAUTIFUL

"O beautiful for spacious skies,
For amber waves of grain,
For purple mountain majesties
Above the fruited plain.
America! America!
God shed His grace on thee.
And crown thy good with brotherhood
From sea to shining sea."

—Katharine Lee Bates, 1893

LIFT EVERY VOICE AND SING

"Lift every voice and sing
Till earth and heaven ring,
Ring with the harmonies of Liberty;
Let our rejoicing rise

High as the listening skies,
Let it resound loud as the rolling sea.
Sing a song full of the faith that the dark past has
taught us,
Sing a song full of the hope that the present has
brought us.
Facing the rising sun of a new day begun
Let us march on till victory is won."

—James Weldon Johnson, 1900

GLOSSARY OF TERMS

Advocate

n.   1. One who argues for a cause; a supporter or defender.

2. One who pleads on another's behalf; an intercessor.

3. One who pleads the cause of another before a tribunal or judicial court.

v.   To speak, plead or argue in favor of an idea.

Affiliate

n.   To be an associate, member, or be connected.

African American

n.   Most African Americans use the term, "African American," to refer to their African slave ancestors and to their descendents, who, although born in America and strove to be "American," were denied full rights of citizenship for hundreds of years until the1950s.

Today, the term is also used to refer to a positive identification with the African background of one's ethnic group heritage, and an increasing awareness of the fact that throughout American history African Americans have played important roles to help make America the nation that it is today.

Also, the term African American when used as a group reference has far less racial overtones when compared to the use of the term "Black American."

Nevertheless, there are still some African Americans, and many more white Americans, who continue to use the term "Black" to refer to African Americans either as individuals or a group. Frequently, this is still the usage for most mainstream media. Perhaps expediency has a greater value for them than enlightened communication.

Allegation

n.　1. An assertion made without proof.

　　2. To declare something is without proof.

Antony, Mark

n.　Mark Antonius (Antony) was a general who succeeded Emperor Julius Caesar. Antony's love affair with Egypt's Queen Cleopatra diminished his triumvirate connection with generals Octavian and Lepidus. As a result, Octavian's armed forces attacked the forces of Antony and Cleopatra and defeated them. In the aftermath both Antony and Cleopatra committed suicide.

Apache

n.　Any member of the Athapaskan tribes in the southwestern U.S. and Mexico that fought many battles with U.S. armed forces from 1861-86. Geronimo was their great warrior chief who was eventually captured, and the Apache tribe was forced to settle in the Oklahoma Territory.

Arduous

adj.　Difficult or hard to do.

Articulate

v.　Expressing one's thoughts and ideas clearly.

Artillery

n.　1. Guns, cannons, tanks, weapon carriers, mechanical machines and apparatuses of all kinds used in war and other situations requiring the use of force.

　　2. The branch of an army that specializes in the use of such weapons.

　　　　　　　　　　　　　　　The African American Quiz Book

Assimilation

n. 1. The process (voluntary or involuntary) wherein a minority group gradually adopts the customs, attitudes, ideas, life style, and values of the prevailing dominant group culture.

2. The process of incorporating and absorbing into the mind.

3. The process of making similar; causing to resemble.

Barbados

n. Island in the Caribbean Sea (West Indies) that became a part of the British colonies in the 1600s and was a major slave center for buying and selling slaves going to the South and North American mainlands.

B.C.E.

Abbreviation for the term Before the Common Era or Before the Christ and the Christian Era, and designating or marking the beginning of a significant time period.

Blacks, "Quasi-Free"

n. African Americans who were free persons, but whose rights and privileges were not recognized and respected to the same extent as free white persons.

Buck

n. 1. Robust or high-spirited young man who might be perceived as stubborn, obstinate, and/or overly aggressive in some way.

2. The lowest rank in a specified military organization. The "Bucks" of America referred to an all African American fighting unit during the American Revolutionary War.

3. A male adult of some animals such as deer, antelope, and rabbit.

Casualty

n.   One injured or killed in an accident, during war or the result of terrorism.

Caustically

adv. Making sharp, cutting remarks about someone or something.

C.E.

Abbreviation for the time period or era coinciding with the birth of Jesus Christ, and the beginning of the Christian Era or Common Era. Previously designated as A.D. and meaning in Latin, "in the year of our Lord."

Caesar, Julius

n.   Julius Caesar, also known as "Gaius," was one of Rome's greatest conquering generals, rulers and statesmen. In 48 B.C., he invaded Egypt, fell in love with Cleopatra, and installed her as his queen. When he eventually returned to Rome he was brutally assassinated by the republic's senators. He fathered two sons by Cleopatra.

Cessation

n.   A ceasing or discontinuance, as of action, whether temporary or final; a stop; a bringing or coming to an end.

Chattel

n.   During the period of institutional slavery in the U.S., it was any tangible, movable property, such as goods, money, or even slaves that someone had a legal right to own. Today, in the U.S. an automobile, furniture, and real estate are examples of chattel property.

Cheyenne

n.   A Native American Indian tribe whose members in the 1800s were noted for being excellent horseman and buffalo hunters. Along with other tribes living in the Great Plains they put up fierce resistance to white settlers encroaching on their land.

Cleopatra

n.   Egyptian queen (69-30 B.C.) noted for her ability as ruler, her beauty, and her charisma. Two Roman generals, Julius Caesar and Mark Antony, were attracted to her and fathered sons by her.

Colonization

n.   The act or process of moving to and settling in a distant territory but still remaining closely associated, by following similar laws, with the parent country.

Common Law

n.   1. In general, a rule of being or conduct; a controlling regulation.
2. The system of laws originated and developed in England and based on court decisions, customs, and usages rather that written laws.
3. English Common Law has greatly influenced the basis for American law.

Compensation

n.   Something, such as money, given or received as payment or reparation as for service or loss.

Congregation

n.   The members of a specific religious group that regularly worship at a church or synagogue.

"Coon"

n. Ethnic slur used by racists, particularly in the slave South, to demean African American people. Comparable in use to such terms as: nigger, jigaboo, spade, darkie, and wild and wooly.

Cooper

n. Craftsman who makes or repairs wooden barrels or tubs that were extremely important for storing various kinds of food, products and liquid beverages like wine and beer.

Comanche

n. A nomadic tribe of the Shoshone family of Native Americans who formerly lived between Wyoming and the Mexican border but are now chiefly in Oklahoma. Historically, they were characterized as warlike and noted for plundering and cruelty toward other tribes as well as whites.

Commend

v. 1. To express approval of, to give praise and recommend as worthy.

2. To commit to the care of another; to entrust.

Confederacy

n. 1. The eleven southern states that separated themselves from the rest of the United States in 1861.

2. A union of political organizations.

Congress

n   1.   A formal assembly of representatives, as of various states, to discuss issues and take steps to solve the nation's problems.

2. The national legislative body of a nation, especially a republic.

3. a.   The national legislative body of the United States consisting of the Senate and the House of Representatives.

b.   The two-year session of this legislature between elections of the House of Representatives.

Constitution

n.   a.   The system of fundamental laws and principles that prescribes the nature, functions, and limits of a government or another institution.

b. The document in which such a system is recorded.

c. The fundamental structure of federal government and law of the United States formed in 1787, ratified in 1789 and variously amended since then.

Convert

v.   1. To change from one form or use to another.

n.   A person who has become a member of a new or different religious group than was the case previously.

Dark Skinned

adj.   Dark skin color. A term used to refer to a person whose skin color is perceived to be darker than that of the majority of the racial group of the society. In the U.S., a term usually applied to persons of African racial descent. Asians, African, and Europeans may also use the term on an intragroup or intergroup basis.

     "Light skinned" has the opposite meaning, with emphasis on appearing to be white or of European descent.

Dehumanize

v.   1. To deprive a person or a group of their natural or God-given human qualities such as: life, freedom, respect and kindness, and pursuit of happiness.

2. The European and American enslavement of the African, and the Nazis systematic brutal treatment and killing of Jews in Europe before and during World War II (the Holocaust) are horrendous examples of dehumanization.

3. 21st-century incidents of the mistreatment and killing of individuals and groups who are victimized by war, terrorists and the like are object of dehumanization.

Demeaning

adj.   To use a word or phrase that degrades or lower the value of a perosn, group, or something.

Denomination

n   In religion, a term used to refer to a division or class of religious organizations that share some common beliefs and practices such as the following Protestant denominations: Baptists, Congregationalists, Episcopalians, Methodists and Presbyterians. All have separate and major differences in certain aspects of their organizational structure, theology and practices.

Derogatory

adj.   A reference term used to belittle the physical or other characteristics of a person or group. Examples: honky, broad, fagot, gook.

Dignitary

n.   1. A person who holds a position of respect and honor because of holding a high rank in religion, government, education or some highly recognized institution.

2. A person worthy of honor and high esteem by others.

Disdain

v.   1. Lack of respect accompanied by a feeling of intense dislike.

2. Behavior and communication that indicates lack of respect by patronizing a person and interacting with them as though they are beneath one's social position.

Disembark

v.   To leave or get off an aircraft, train, ship or some other mode of transportation and be on land.

Disfranchise

v.   To deprive of a privilege, an immunity, or right of citizenship especially the right to vote.

Disparage

v.   To speak in a way that belittles, demeans, and shows disrespect for an individual or a group.

Dominant

adj. 1. Exercising the most influence or control in a situation, a group, a state or even a nation.

2. Most prominent in a position of power and influence, such as a racial, religious, political, gender, or ethnic group.

Dravidians

n.   1. A large dark-skinned population of an ethnic group in southern India and northern Sri Lanka that includes Tamil, Telegu, Malayan, and Kannada language groups.

2. A member of any of the peoples that speak one of the Dravidian languages; especially a member of one of the pre-Indo-European peoples of South India.

Emancipation Proclamation

n.   On January 1, 1863, a military order was issued by President Abraham Lincoln, who was commander in chief of the Union armed forces. It allowed for the admittance of slaves into certain states as "free persons." It did not grant freedom to slaves living in slave states or parts of slave states that were not a part of the Confederacy.

Emigration

n.   1. Removal from or leaving one country or state to go to another for the purpose of taking up residence in the new place.

2. An emigrant is a person who leaves his country and travels to another country to take up residence there.

Ethnic Minority Group

n.   A distinctive cultural group in the larger society that tends to have a smaller population and influence compared to that society's dominant group.

Ethnocentrism

n.   1. The assumption and the attitude, conscious or unconscious, that one's own culture, society, ethnicity, race, or nation is superior to others.

2. Cultural anthropologists state that all human beings are ethnocentric to a greater or lesser degree depending on the cultural environment they have been raised in.

Ethnologist

n.   An anthropologist who scientifically studies certain aspects of human culture such as language, life style, beliefs, taboos, and technology for the purpose of gaining knowledge and making predictions about them.

European Americans

n.   Americans whose ancestors originated in various countries in Europe.

Expedite

v.   To hasten, speed up the action, progress or procedure to complete a task.

Expedition

n.   1. a. A journey undertaken by a group of people with a definite objective

b. The group undertaking such a journey.

2. Speed in performance; promptness

Facilitate

v.   To make easy or easier; to free from difficulty or to lessen the labor or task of doing something.

Forerunner

n. 1. A person who goes before or announces the coming of another.

2. An indication of the approach of something or someone similar in time.

3. The Magi who traveled to Bethlehem in Judea to present gifts to the baby Jesus were forerunners of a great event as mentioned in the Bible and the Qur'an.

Formidable

adj. Very impressive in size and appearance, or in some other way.

Free Black

n. An African American who, during the period of slavery, was not held in bondage, had certain rights, and was relatively free.

Freedman

n. A former slave who was manumitted or freed from the bondage of slavery.

Free State

n. 1. One of the original thirteen colonies making up the New England states.

2. Any state prohibiting slavery prior to the American Civil War.

Fugitive

n. 1. A person who flees or has fled from some kind of danger.

2. A slave who has escaped from bondage.

Genealogy

n.   1. A detailed record or table of the direct lineage or descent of a person, family, or group from an ancestor or ancestors.

2. The study or investigation of ancestry, a family tree and family histories.

Genre

n.   A kind or type.

Groomer

n   One who cares for horses. Many slaves cared for their owner's horses by regularly brushing and washing them, and trimming their hoofs.

Heathen

n   1. Term used by many European Christian conquerors and colonists for many centuries for the non-Christian people with whom they came into contact.

2. One who is regarded as irreligious, uncivilized, a pagan, and religiously or spiritually unenlightened.

Homestead

n.   1. The land and place where a person or family locates their home and other physical assets.

2. The U.S. Homestead Act of 1862 granted up to 160 acres of land to settlers to develop farms.

Hun

n. 1. A nomadic people of northern Asia who, in the fifth century under military leadership of Attila, the "Hun," invaded and conquered
a great part of Europe and Asia.

2. Has been used as a disparaging term for people of German descent.

Ideology

n. 1. The body of ideas reflecting the social needs and aspirations of an
individual, group, culture or nation.

2. A set of beliefs that form the basis of a political, economic, or
other system.

Immigrant

n. A person who comes to a country where they were not born in order
to settle there.

Impunity

n. Free or exempt from punishment after committing a crime.

Immigration

n. Coming or moving into another country or nation different from
your place of birth either voluntarily or involuntarily, and becoming
a permanent resident willingly or unwillingly.

Incarceration

v. To put a person in jail or prison for a crime that was committed.

Incivility

n. 1. Not showing ordinary courtesy, politeness or civil behavior toward another person or group. Being rude.

2. Members of minority groups have often been victims of incivility.

Indentured Servant

n. A person under contract to provide service to another for a specified period of time, usually 3, 5 or 7 years. Hundreds of Irish and British indentured servants worked in the English colonies.

Indignant

adj. Expressing displeasure, scorn, or anger because of an unjust act of mistreatment.

Indomitable

adj. Not easily defeated, discouraged or subdued.

Indigenous

adj. A native of or naturally belonging to a country (nation) or region.

Indulge

v. To yield to or satisfy the desires of oneself or another. Parents are sometimes accused of pampering or spoiling their children.

Indulgence

n. In the 1500s, some members in the Roman Catholic Church believed they could receive remission of sin(s) and freedom from punishment by purchasing an "indulgence." Martin Luther, a Roman Catholic priest and theologian, protested this practice, and led a movemen that became known as the Protestant Reformation.

Ingenious

adj 1. Marked by independence and creativity in thought or action.

2. Showing inventiveness and skill.

3. Benjamin Banneker (1731-1806), a free African American, was a noted mathematician, astronomer and ingenious clock maker. Because of his surveying abilities he was selected by George Washington and Thomas Jefferson to be a key member of the surveying team to lay out the grid for streets and construction in the new capital, Washington, D.C.

Iniquity

n. A situation, circumstance, and condition within a society that systematically treats a person or group unjustly.

Immigrant

adj. Inborn qualities or hereditary characteristics.

Institutional

adj. 1. Activities, programs relating to an established organization for the purpose of obtaining particular objectives (economic, educational, political, social, or religious).

2. Characteristics or suggestive of an institution, especially in being uniform and systemic.

Interracial Hybridization

n.   1. A new genetically racial population that has resulted because of the interbreeding between two or more genetically different human populations.

2. Obvious examples are the diverse Hispanic/Latino populations of Mexico, Latin America, and South America that have resulted because of Spanish and Portuguese interbreeding with various indigenous Native American Indian tribes with whom they came into contact.

Another example are the offspring of European white American and African American interbreeding that has taken place in the United States for more that 300 years. Although some of these offspring may physically appear to be white or have light complexions, they can in fact have a significant number of African genes as well as European except for skin color. The same can be said for many African Americans who outwardly may not appear to be of stereotypical European white descent but who may have considerable genes from that population group.

There is a growing trend for many persons in the U.S. who are of mixed racial ancestry wanting to be designated as "bi-racial," especially on U.S. Census data, and some who refer to themselves as "blended."

Jamaica

n.   An island in the Caribbean Sea south of Cuba. Originally inhabited by Arawak Indians, first visited by Columbus in the 1490s, and settled by the Spanish in 1509. The British captured the island in 1655 and it became an important African slave center for the British in marketing and "seasoning" slaves.

Jim Crow

adj. In the late 1800s, a term used to refer to the racial laws and practices segregating African Americans from white Americans and discriminating on that basis. Separate drinking fountains and restrooms for African Americans were required as well as for whites.

Lin Jin

n. A leading geneticist in the People's Republic of China.

Kunte Kinte

n. One of the main characters of Alex Haley's book "Roots." He was kidnapped as a youth from his tribe in West Africa. He was a member of the Mandingo tribe and was of Muslim religious background.

Liberia

n. A country of western Africa on the Atlantic Ocean. It was founded in 1821 through the efforts of the American Colonization Society and settled mainly by freed slaves from 1822-1860s. Liberia is the oldest independent nation in Africa, established in 1847. A military coup in 1980 initiated a period of despotic government and civil unrest leading to full-scale civil war in 1990. A cease-fire agreement was reached in 1996.

Loyalist

n. Term used to refer to a person who is loyal in their allegiance (especially in times of revolt) as during the American Revolutionary period. Those who supported the British against the Americans were considered "loyalists."

Majority

n.   1. The greater number or part; a number more than half of the total.

2. The number of votes over half of those cast.

3. In nations or situations involving both majority and minority groups, ethnic, racial or political, it is the group that has the greater power to influence and control the relationships between the two groups.

Mammy

n.   A term used to refer to a female African American slave who was a nursemaid, who suckled infants, especially for white mothers who could not provide adequate breast milk for their children. Today, it is considered an offensive term by African Americans.

Manumission

n.   The formal act of a slave owner of freeing a slave from bondage.

Master or Slavemaster

n.   The owner of a person or persons held as a slave who were considered the personal or "chattel" property of the owner.

Midwife

n.   A person, usually a woman, who is trained to assist women in childbirth. Many African American women provided this service for the birth of both white and Black babies during slavery and afterwards.

Militant

adj. 1. Aggressive or hostile in attitude or actions, especially in defense of a cause.

2. Waging war; fighting; warring.

Minority

n   1. a. The smaller in number of two or more groups forming a whole.

b. A group or party having fewer than an effective number of votes.

2 a. An ethnic, racial, religious or other group having a distinctive presence in a society.

b. A group having little power or representation relative to other groups in a society.

3. Being under a certain legal age and not entitled to certain adult rights and privileges.

Monetary

adj. Of or relating to money.

Mockery

n.   The act of making fun of a person or a group by false and stereotypical imitations, taunting, and deriding.

Monotheism

n.   The belief that there is only one universal God. For Jews, "Yahweh," for Christians, "God," and for Muslims, "Allah."

Mulatto

n.   A term of Spanish origin which was commonly used to refer to a racially-mixed person of African and European ancestry, and who has a skin color and other physical features reflecting such a mixture. Now considered an offensive term. Some use the term "bi-racial" to refer to a person of mixed racial ancestry, but this term is also offensive to some.

Mystic

adj.   1. Beyond human comprehension; baffling human understanding; obscure; mysterious.

2. A number of religious leaders such as Gautama Siddhartha, founder of Buddhism, Abraham of Judaism, Jesus of Christianity, Muhammad of Islam, and Nanak of Sikhism, all believed they had mystical experiences.

3. Of or relating to religious mysteries or occult rites and practices.

Myth

n.   1. In religion it is a traditional, typically ancient story with supernatural beings and heroes that serves as a fundamental explanation of how a group of people in that society tend to view the world in terms of history, purpose, and the future.

2. A fiction or half-truth that becomes a part of conventional culture For example, Halloween witches and Santa Claus and reindeer.

Musket

n.   A long-barreled muzzle-loading shoulder gun used from the 1600s-1800s that shot lead pellets of different sizes and velocities.

Mongrel

n.   1. An animal or plant resulting from various inter-breeding, especially a dog of mixed undetermined breed.

2. A cross between different breeds, groups, or varieties, especially a mixture that is or appears to be incongruous.

3. A derogatory term frequently used by racists and neo-racists to refer to the offspring of parents having different racial and/or ethnic backgrounds.

Monticello

n.   An estate of central Virginia southeast of the city of Charlottesville. Designed by Thomas Jefferson, it was founded in 1770 and was his home for fifty-six years and is now a national shrine.

Mount Vernon

n.   An estate located in northeast Virginia on the Potomac River near Washington, D.C. It was the home of George Washington from 1752 until his death in 1799. The mansion, built in 1743 by Lawrence Washington, George's half-brother, has been restored and is open to the public as a national shrine.

Mongol

n.   Of or relating to an ancient region of east-central Asia called Mongolia. Genghis Khan united the Mongol tribes of the region in the 1300s. After the 1700s China and Russia contended for control of the area with the southern part eventually joining China.

Moors

n.   1.   a.   Members of a Muslim people of mixed Berber, African, and Arab descent, now living chiefly in northwest Africa.

b.   Term used to refer to the Muslims who invaded Spain in the eighth century and established a civilization in Andalusia that lasted until the late fifteenth century.

c.   Term used in the English language for many centuries to refer to a dark-skinned person. For example, Othello is referre to as the "the Moor" in Shakespeare's drama.

New Netherlands

n.   A Dutch colony established in North America near the Hudson and Delaware rivers. Referred to as New Amsterdam until the British took over the territory in 1664 and called it "New York."

Non-Violence

n.   1.   Not using abusive, aggressive, or unjust exercise of power for the purpose of bringing about economic, political, or social change of some kind.

2.   Some examples of non-violence techniques used during the 1950-'60s Civil Rights period included informational picketing, demonstration marches, passive resistance, and "sit-ins."

3.   Mohandas Gandhi of India and Dr. Martin Luther King, Jr., advocated the use of non-violence to help bring about social change.

Northwest Expedition

n.   A term used interchangeably with "Northwest Passage" to refer to the Meriwether Lewis and William Clark expedition (1804-6) to the Northwest.

Nova Scotia

n.   1. A province of eastern Canada comprising a mainland peninsula and the adjacent Cape Breton Island.

2. Following the American Revolution, hundreds of free African Americans and slaves who had taken sides with the British ("Loyalists") against the Americans, fled to Nova Scotia for safety and to receive land promised to them.

3. During the 1800s, many Scottish people also immigrated to the region, leading to its name, which is the Latin version of New Scotland.

Nuance

n.   A slight, delicate variation in meaning for a word, sound, or tone.

Olmecs

n.   An early Mesoamerican Indian civilization centered in the Vera Cruz region of southeast Mexico that flourished between 1300-1400 BC, whose cultural ancestors are believed to be African by some scholars. Their influence was widespread throughout southern Mexico and Central America.

Pacification

v.   Actions taken for purpose of making or maintaining peace between potentially hostile or warring parties.

Pacifism

n.   1. Opposition to the use of force under any circumstances.

2. Consientious objectors to war or military activities are often pacificts.

Paleoanthropologist

n.   Scientist who specializes in the study of early forms of fossil humans.

Paleontologist

n.   Scientist who specializes in the study of life forms existing in prehistoric or geological times, represented by the fossils of plants, animals, and other organisms.

"Pass"

adj. 1. Term generally used to refer to those African Americans whose light skin color made it possible for them to blend and interact with white persons and not be recognized as having mixed racial ancestry, and to be perceived as white.

2. In the past, many African Americans who "passed" did so in order to avoid white hostility and rejection and as a means of coping.

Passive Resistance

n.   A person who refuses to actively respond to another person's aggressive, abusive, or harmful behavior designed to hurt them in some way.

Patronize

v.   1. To go to as a customer, especially on a regular basis.

2. To treat another person in a condescending manner because of ethnic, racial, gender, age, class, disability, or some other kind of difference.

Pedestrian

n.   One who travels on foot.

adj. Lacking wit or imagination.

Pilgrim

n.   1. A religious devotee who journeys to a shrine or sacred place.

2. One of the English Separatists who founded the colony of Plymouth in New England in 1620.

Pioneer

v.   1. a.   To open up an area or prepare a place for settlement.

b.   To initiate or participate initially in the development of some scientific theory, knowledge, and/or methodology and practice.

adj. 1 a.   Of or relating to or characteristics of early settlers.

b. Leading the way; trailblazing.

Plasma

n.   1. An electrically neutral ionized gas in an electric discharge; distinctly different from solids and liquids and normal gases.

2. Any watery animal fluid.

3. A green, slightly translucent variety of chalcedony used as a gemstone.

4. Fluid portion of milk, from which the curd has been separated by coagulation; whey.

Polytheism

n.   The worship of, or belief in, more that one god or many gods. Hinduism is an example.

Polytheistic

adj. Of or pertaining to polytheism; characterizing polytheism, professing or advocating polytheism.

Potawatomi

n.   A Native American Indian tribe that lived in the lower part of Michigan and adjoining states, especially during the 18th century.

Precipitate

n.   1. To cause to happen, especially suddenly or prematurely.

     2. To cause to condense and fall from the air as rain, snow, sleet, or hail.

     3. To cause a solid substance to be separated from a solution.

adj. Moving rapidly and heedlessly; speeding headlong.

Precocious

adj. Showing unusual early development or maturity, especially pertaining to mental forwardness.

Privateer

n.   A ship privately owned and crewed, but authorized by a government during wartime to attack and capture enemy ships or commanders of such ships.

Procure

v.   To get, obtain, or secure by some effort.

Prominent

adj. 1. Having a quality that thrusts itself into attention; distinguished above others.

     2. Immediately noticeable; conspicuous.

Promiscuous

adj. Engaging in sexual relationships and/or intercourse carelessly and indiscriminately.

Proselytize

v.   To purposely induce someone to convert to one's own religious faith, political beliefs or some other doctrines, and as a result give up one's previous ideas about such matters.

Prototype

n.   An original, full-scale and usually working model of a new product of an existing product.

Pundit

n.   A person who professes to have or who is believed to have knowledge, experience and authority about some matter.

Quest

n.   To seek, search or pursue something like a prize, adventure or answer to a question.

Qur'an (Koran)

n.   Sacred text of the Islamic religion and considered by Muslims to contain the revelations of God to Mohammad, the founder of Islam.

Rationalize

v.   To explain or interpret one's beliefs and behavior, and in some cases to do this on a very subjective and biased view point.

adj. 1. Stubbornly refusing to obey authority, custom and regulations.

       2. Unruly, hard to deal with.

Reconstruction Period

n. Period of time after the U.S. Civil War (1865-1877), when the Union or federal government established policies and implemented programs to politically, economically, and socially rebuild the war-devastated Confederate South, and meet the needs of the people there, especially millions of former slaves.

Redlining

v. The practice of some financial lenders, especially mortgage, to discriminate against certain ethnic and racial minority groups, and not equitably provide them with adequate funding for capital resources, investments, real estate purchases and the like.

Refuge

n. 1. A place of shelter and safety from danger or harm of some kind.

2. A refugee seeks protection from harm.

Relinquish

v. 1. To retire from; give up or abandon.

2. To put aside or desist from.

3. To let go; surrender.

4. To stop holding physically; release.

Restrictive Covenant

n. Prior to the Federal Fair Housing Act of 1968, it was a common real estate practice in most parts of the U.S. to enter into contracts that would prevent members of minority groups (mostly African Americans, Asians, Hispanics and Jews) from buying and renting real estate in predominantly white neighborhoods. The covenant stipulations were almost always enforced by local and state laws even when challenged.

Sanction

n. An individual or group may approve, support, or go along with a particular law, custom, tradition or way of doing things affirmed (sanctioned) by some authority.

Savage

n. A person regarded as primitive or uncivilized; brutal, fierce, or vicious.

adj. Not domesticated or cultivated; wild.

Sectarian

adj. Devoted to a particular religious denomination or sect to the exclusion of others.

Attitude may be based on "blind" dogmatism for some, and on reasonable and rational belief and understanding for others.

Seditious

adj. To participate in activities (covert or overt) considered to arouse opposition to lawful authority and inciting extreme dissent.

Segregate

v. To require, compel or force the separation of a group, race, or class from others in the situation or society.

Senegal

n. A country of western Africa on the Atlantic Ocean. Wolof and other West Atlantic peoples settled the coast, while the interior formed part of the medieval empires of Ghana, Mali, and Songhai. Senegal was awarded to France in 1815 by the Treaty of Paris and became a French colony in 1895 as part of French West Africa, with full independence being won in 1960.

Sioux

n. A very large population of Native American Indian tribes, sometimes referred to collectively as the Dakota. They have inhabited the northern Great Plains from Minnesota to eastern Montana, and from Saskatchewan in Canada to Nebraska. Today, they are located mainly in South and North Dakota.

Slave Mistress

A slave woman who was coerced by her owner or other whites in his family or employ to have sexual relations.

Slave State

n. Any of the fifteen states in which slavery was legal before the Civil War, including Alabama, Arkansas, Delaware, Florida, Georgia, Kentucky, Louisiana, Mississippi, Maryland, Missouri, North Carolina, South Carolina, Tennessee, Texas, and Virginia.

Socioeconomic

adj. Of or involving both social and economic aspects of something.

Solomon, King

n. The son of King David in Biblical history. Under his reign (961-922 B.C.E.) he built the first Jewish Temple in Jerusalem, and he was passionately in love with Queen Sheba of Egypt.

Spiritual

adj. 1. Relating to things of spirit or soul and expressed in human behavior by actions which are considered unselfish, loving, caring, moral, and divine-like.

2. Having the nature of spirit; not tangible or material.

3. Concerning or affecting the soul.

4. Genre or type of African American religious music.

Statutory

adj. Authorized, fixed by established law.

Stereotypes

n.   A conventional, formulaic, and oversimplified conception, opinion, or image.

Stipulation

n.   1. The act of bargaining or making an agreement.

2. Any particular article, item or condition in a mutual agreement.

Subordination

n.   The act of being placed into a lower or inferior class, rank or social position.

Sub-Saharan

adj. Of or relating to or located in the region of Africa south of the Sahara, and often referred to as "Black Africa."

Subtleties

n.   Having the quality of being a fine distinction in meaning of a word or idea.

Surrogate

n.   One who substitutes or replaces another person such as a foster mother.

Synthesis

n.   The combination of separate elements of thought into a whole, as of simple into complex conceptions, species into a genus, individual propositions into systems.

Tamils

n. A member of a Dravidian people of southern India and northern Sri Lanka.

Tangible

adj. That which has substance and has perceived value.

Tenacity

n. 1. Persistent, determined, doesn't give in or give up easy.

2. Some human diseases like cancer and AIDS are very tenacious.

Theology

n. The systematic study of the nature of God and religious truth; rational inquiry into religious questions.

Therapeutic

adj. Functioning to help or cure a physical, psychological, or spiritual disease or combination of thereof.

Tom

n. 1. The male of various animals, especially a male cat or turkey.

2. "Uncle Tom" is a term used mostly in the past by some to refer to an African American male whose behavior toward whites is usually overly servile, flattering and uncritical.

3. The main character in Harriet Beecher Stowe's pre-Civil War novel, "Uncle Tom's Cabin," was characterized with this kind of behavior.

Trailblazer

n. An innovative leader in a field; pioneer.

Turban

n. A traditionally Muslim headdress consisting of a long scarf of linen, cotton, or silk that is wound around a small cap or directly around the head.

Unscrupulous

adj. 1. Oblivious to or contemptuous of what is morally and ethically right.

2. Dishonorable and unprincipled regarding the highest core values of American culture.

Valet

n. 1. A man's male servant, who takes care of his clothes and performs other personal services.

2. An employee, as in a hotel or on a ship, or a parking lot attendant, who performs personal services for guests, passengers, and the car owner.

REFERENCES, SELECTED READING AND STUDY RESOURCES

The following titles were of immense value to the authors. They are recommended to others who may wish to study African American History.

BOOKS:

Abdul-Jabar, Kareem and Steinberg, Alan, "Black Profiles in Courage," New York: William Morrow & Co., 1996

Adams, Russell L. "Great Negroes of the Past and Present," Chicago: Afro-American Publishing Co., 1969

Aldrich, Gene, "The Black Heritage of Oklahoma," Edmond, OK: Thompson Book and Supply Co., 1973

Ali, Muhammad, "The Greatest: My Own Story, "New York: Random House, 1975

Angelo, Maya, "I Know Why The Caged Bird Sings," New York: Bantam Books, Inc., 1970

Appiah, Kwame A. and Gates. Louis G., eds., "Africana, The Encyclopedia of the African and African American Experience," New York: Basic Civitas Books, 1999

Aptheker, Bettina,"The Morning Breaks: The Trial of Angela Davis," New York: International Publishers, 1975

Aptheker, Herbert, "A Documentary History of the Negro in the United States," Secaucus, New Jersey: The Citadel Press, 1974

Asante, Molefi K., "Afrocentricity," Trenton, New Jersey: Africa World Press, Inc., 1992

Asante, Molefi K., and Mattson, Mark T., "Historical and Cultural Atlas of African Americans," New York: Macmillan Publishing Co., 1992

Austin, Alan D., "African Muslims in Ante Bellum America," Garland Publishing, Inc.

Baldwin, James, "Go Tell It On The Mountain," New York: Dell Publishing

Inc., 1952

Ball, Edward, "Slaves in the Family," New York: Farrar, Straus & Giroux, 1998

Balmer, Randall, "Blessed Assurance: A History of Evangelicalism in America," Boston: Beacon Press Publishers, 1970

Banks, James A., "Teaching the Black Experience," Belmont, CA: Fearon Publishers, 1970

Barboza, Steven, "The African American Book of Values," New York: Bantam Doubleday Dell Publishing Group, Inc., 1996

Barrett, Lenard E., "Soul-Force," Garden City, NY: Anchor Press/Doubleday, 1974

Baughman, E. Earl, "Black Americans," New York: Academic Press, 1971

Bennett, Lerone, "Pioneers in Protest," New York: Penguin Books, 1968

Bennett, Lerone, "Before the Mayflower," New York: Penguin Books, 1986

Berry, Mary F. and Blassingame, John W., "Long Memory: The Black Experience in America," New York: Oxford University Press, 1982

Berkey, Johnathon, "The Foundation of Islam, Religion and Society in the Near East, 600-1800,: Cambridge: Cambridge University Press, 2003

Billingsley, Andrew, "Climbing Jacob's Ladder: The Enduring Legacy of African American Families," New York: Simon & Schuster, 1992

Block, Charles et.al., "Pictorial Encyclopedia: People Who Made America," Skokie, ILL: United States Historical Society, Inc., 1978

Blockson, Charles L., "Black Genealogy," Baltimore, MD: Black Classic Press, 1991

Boyd, Herb, "Down the Glory Road," New York: Avon Books, 1995

Brodie, James, M., "Created Equal: The Lives and Ideas of Black American Innovators," New York: William Morrow and Co. Inc., Bill Adler Books, 1993

Buckley, Gail, "American Patriots: The Story of Blacks in the Military from the Revolution to Desert Storm," New York: Random House, 2001

Carmichael, Stokely and Hamilton, Charles V., "Black Power:The Politics of Liberation in America," New York: Vintage Books, 1967

Carrington, John F. "Talking Drums of Africa," New York: Negro University, 1969

Castillo, George R., My Life Between The Cross and the Bars," Shalimar, FL: G & M Publications, 1996

Chan, Sucheng , ed. Et.al., "Peoples of Color in the American West," Massachusetts: D.C. Heath and Company, 1994

Chase, Henry, "In Their Footsteps: The American Visions Guide to African-American Heritage Sites," New York: Henry Holt and Company, 1994

Chideya, Farai, "Don't Believe the Hype: Fighting Cultural Information about African Americans," New York: Plume/Penguin Books, USA, Inc.

Christmas, Walter, ed., "Negro Heritage Library," Vols. I and II, New York: American Book-Stratford Press, 1964-66

Clark, Kenneth B., "Dark Ghetto," New York: Harper Torchbooks, 1965.

Clayton, Ed., "Martin Luther King: The Peaceful Warrior," New York: An Archway Paperback, 1969

Collins, Charles M. and Cohen, David, "African Americans: A Celebration of Achievement," New York: Penguin Books USA Inc., 1995

Collum, Danny D., "African Americans in the Spanish Civil War," New York: G.K. Hall & Co., 1992

Cool J, LL, "And the Winner Is…" New York: Scholastic, Inc., 2002

Combs, Milton A., "Ethnic Groups in the History of California," Sausalito, CA: Suisun College, rev. 1992

Combs, Milton A., "E Plurbis Unumi: Teaching Multicultural Education," Scholia, Suisun, CA: Solano College, 1994

Cone, James, "For My People: Black Theology and the Black Church," Maryknoll, NY: Orbis Books, 1988

Cowan, Tom and Maguire, Jack, "Timelines of African-American History: 500 Years of Black Acheivement," New York: Roundtable Press, 1994

Curtis, Edward, "Islam in Black America: Identity, Liberation, and Difference in African-American Islamic Thought," New York: State University Press, 2003

Dannin, Robert, "Black Pilgrimage to Islam," New York: Oxford University Press, 2003

Davis, Benjamin O. Jr., "American," Washington D.C.: Smithsonian Institution Press, 1991

Davis, Burke, "Black Heroes of the American Revolution," New York: Harcourt Brace Jovanovich, 1976

Dubois, W.E.B. "The Souls of Black Folk," New York: Signet Classic, 1982

Dyson, Michael, "Between God and Gangsta Rap," New York: Oxford

University Press, 1996

Ellison, Ralph, "Invisible Man," New York: Signet/Random House, 1947

Esposito, John L., "Islam: The Straight Path," New York: Oxford University Press, 1998

Evanz, Karl, "The Messenger: The Rise and Fall of Elijah Muhammad," New York: Pantheon Books, 1999

Farrakhan, Louis, "A Torchlight for America," Chicago: FCN Publishing Co., 1993

Favors, John and Kathryne, "Every Teacher's Guidebook on Thematic Integrated Education," Sacramento, CA: Jonka Enterprises, 1994

Fogel, Robert W., Engerman, Stanley L., "Time On The Cross," New York: W.W. Norton & Company, 1989

Feagin, Joe R. and Feagin, Clairece B., "Racial and Ethnic Relations," Upper Saddle River, NJ: Prentice Hall, 1999

Forbes, Jack D., "Africans and Native Americans: The Language of Race and the Evolution of Red-Black Peoples," Chicago: University of Illinois Press, 1993

Felder, Cain H., "Troubling Biblical Waters: Race, Class and the Family," New York: Maryknoll Orbis Books, 1989

Fishel, Leslie H. and Quarles, Benjamin, "The Black American," Glenview, Ill.: Scott, Forsman, and Company, 1976

Franklin, John H. ed., "Color and Race," Boston: Houghton Mifflin Co., 1968

Franklin, John H. and Moss, Alfred A., "From Slavery to Freedom, A History of Negro Americans" New York: Alfred A. Knopf, Inc., 1988

Frazier, E. Franklin, "The Negro Church in America," New York: Schocken Books, 1963

Garrow, David J., "Bearing the Cross," New York: Vintage Books, 1988

Gentry, Curt, "J. Edgar Hover: The Man and The Secrets," New York: Penguin Books, 1992

George, Nelson, "Hip Hop America," New York: Penguin USA, 1999

Ginzberg, Eli and Eichner, Alfred S., "The Troublesome Presence," New York: Mentor Books, 1966

Goldsby, Richard A., "Race and Races," New York: Macmillan Publishing Co., 1977

Goodheart, Lawrence B., Brown, Richard D., and Rabe, Stephen G., eds.,

---

"Slavery in American Society," Lexington, Mass: D.C. Heath and Company, 1976

Graves, Curtis M. and Hodges, Jane A., "Famous Black Americans: Folder Games for the Classroom," Silver Springs, MD: Bartleby Press, 1986

Gregory, Dick, "No More Lies: The Myth and Reality of American History," New York: Harper & Row, 1971

Griessman, B. Eugene, "Diversity: Challenges and Opportunities," New York: HarperCollins, 1993

Guralnik, David B. ed., "Webster's New World Dictionary," New York: Simon & Schuster, 1984

Gutman, Herbert, "The Black Family in Slavery and Freedom: 1750-1925," New York: Pantheon Press, 1976

Haddad, Yvonne Y., "Islamic Values in the United States," New York: Oxford University Press, 1987

Haley, Alex, "Roots," New York: Doubleday and Company, 1976

Hanes, Colonel B.C., "Bill Pickett: Bulldogger," Norman, OK: University of Oklahoma Press, 1989

Harlan, Louis R., "Booker T. Washington in Perspective," Jackson, MS: University of Mississippi, 1998

Harding, Vincent, "There Is A River, The Black Struggle for Freedom in America," New York: Vintage Books, 1983

Henderson, Julie, "Educating for Democracy," Stanford University Dissertation, Palo Alto, CA, 2004

Hill, James L., "The Saw Mill: An Autobiographical," Mary Esther, FL: JBH Publishers, 2002

Hochschild, Adam, "Bury the Chains: Prophets and Rebels in the Fight to Free an Empire's Slaves," New York: Houghton Mifflin Co., 2005

Hudson, Wade and Valerie W. Wesley, "Afro-Bets, Book of Black Heroes, From A to Z," Orange, NJ: 1988

Hughes, Langston, "The Langston Hughes Reader: The Selected Writings of Langston Hughes," New York: George Braziller, Inc., 1958

Hurston, Zora Neale, "Dust Tracks On The Road," New York: HarperCollins, 1970

Igus, Toyami, ed., Book of Black Heroes, Great Women in the Struggle,"

Orange, NJ: Just Us Books, 1991

Jakes, T.D., "He-Motions," New York: G.P. Putnam's Sons, 2004

Johnson, Jesse, J., "The Black Soldier Documented (1619-1815)," Hampton, VA: Hampton Institute, 1969

Katz, William K., "Eyewitness: The Negro in American History," New York: Pitman Publishing Corporation, 1969

Katz, William K., "Black Indians, A Hidden Heritage," New York: Macmillan/ Atheneum, 1986

Katz, William K., "The Black West," New York: Simon & Schuster/ Touchstone, 1996

Knowles, Louis, L. and Prewitt, Kenneth, "Institutional Racism in America," Englewoods Cliff, NJ: Prentice-Hall Inc., 1969

Kranz, Rachel and Kaslow, Philip J., "Biographical Dictionary of African Americans," New York: Checkmark Books, 1999

Lasartemay, Eugene P. and Rudge, Mary, "For Love of Jack London," New York: Vantage Press, Inc., 1991

Leakey, Richard and Lewin, Roger, "Origins Reconsidered: In Search of What Makes a Human," New York: Doubleday, 1992

Levine, Lawrence W., "Black Culture and Black Consciousness," New York: The Oxford University Press, 1977

Libby, Jean, "From Slavery to Salvation," Jackson MS: University Press of Mississippi, 1994

Light, Alan, "Vibe History of Hip Hop," New York: Random House, Inc., 1999

Lincoln, C. Eric. "The Black Muslims in America," Boston: Beacon Press, 1973

Lincoln, C. Eric and Mamiya, Lawrence H. "The Black Church in the African American Experience," Durham, NC: Duke University Press, 1990

Litwack, Leon F., "Been in the Storm So Long: The Aftermath of Slavery," New York: Vintage Books, 1980

Lommel, Cookie, "History of Hip Hop," Broomall, PA: Chelsea House Publishers, 2001

Low, W, Augustus and Clift, Virgil A., "Encyclopedia of Black America," New York: McGraw-Hill, Inc./Da Capo Press, 1981

Marable, Manning, "How Capitalism Underdeveloped Black America," Boston, MA: South End Press, 1983

Marable, Manning, "W.E.B. DuBois: Black Radical Democrat,"
Boston: Twayne Publishers, 1986

Marden, Charles F., et al. "Minorities in American Society," New York: Harper
Collins Publishers, 1992

Marlowe, Gertrude W., "A Right Worthy Grand Mission: Maggie Lena Walker
And the Quest For Black Economic Empowerment," Washington, DC:
Howard University Press, 2004

McCall, Nathan, "What's Going On," New York: Random House, 1997

McCloud, Aminah B., "African American Islam," New York: Routledge, 1995

McMickle, Marvin, "An Encyclopedia of African American Christian Heritage,"
Valley Forge, PA: Judson Press, 2002

McPherson, James M., "The Negro's Civil War," New York: Ballatine Books,
1991

Meir, August and Rudwick, Elliott M., "From Plantation to Ghetto," New
York: American Book-Stratford Press, Inc., 1996

Meltzer, Milton, "A History of The American Negro," New York: Thomas Y.
Crowell Co., 1964

Metzger, Bruce M. and Murphy, Roland E., eds., "The New Annotated
Bible with the Apocryphal/Deuterocanonical Books," New York: Oxford
University Press, 1994

Mitchell, Henry, "Black Belief," New York: Harper & Row Publishers, 1975

Mitchell, Henry, " Black Church Beginnings " Grand Rapids, MI: Wm. B.
Eerdmans Publishing Co., 2004

Montagu, Ashley, "Statement on Race," New York: Oxford University Press,
1993

Motley, Mary P., The Invisible Soldier: The Experience of the Black Soldier,
World War II," Detroit: Wayne University Press, 1987

Muzorewa, Gwinyai, "The Origins And Development of African Theology,"
Maryknoll, NY: Orbis Books, 1985

Myers, Walter D., "The Greatest: Muhammad Ali," New York: Scholastic Inc., 2001

Myrdal, Gunnar, "An American Dilemma (The Negro Problem and Modern
Democracy)" New York: Harper & Row Publishers, 1944

Nagel, Tilman, "The History of Islamic Theology, From Muhammad to the
Present," Princeton, NJ: Markus Weiner Pub., 2000

Nobles, Wade W., "Africanicity and the Black Familly," Oakland, CA: A Black Family Institute Publication, 1985

Oates, James, "Slavery and Freedom: An Interpretation of the Old South," New York: Vintage Press, 1990

Page, Clarence, "Showing My Color: Impolite Essays on Race and Identity," New York: HarperCollins Publishers, 1996

Painter, Nell Irvin, Standing at Armageddon: The United States, 1877-1919," New York: W.W. Norton & Company, 1987

Painter, Nell Irvin, "Sojourner Truth, A Life, A Symbol," New York: W.W. Norton & Company, 1996

Payne, Wardell, ed.,"Dictionary of African American Religious Bodies," Washington, DC: Howard University, 1995

Pickhall, Marmaduke, M., "The Meaning of the Glorious Koran: An Explanatory Explanation," New York: Mentor Books

Pinkney, Alphonso, "Black Americans," Englewood Cliffs, NJ: Prentice-Hall, Inc., 1987

Pinnington, Richard, "Breaking the Ice: The Racial Integration of Southwest Conference Football," Jefferson, NC: McFarland, 1987

Potter, Joan and Claytor, Constance, "African American Firsts," Elizabeth Town, NY: Pinto Press, 1994

Powell, Colin, "My American Journey," New York: Ballatine Books, 1996

Robinson, Randall, "The Debt: What America Owes to Blacks"

Rogers, J.A., "World's Great Men of Color," New York: Touchstone, 1996

Rose, Tricia, "Black Noise: Rap Music and Black Culture in Contemporary America," Wesleyan University Press, 1994

Rowan, Carl T., "Breaking Barriers: A Memoir," New York: HarperPerennial, 1992

Russell, Dick, "Black Genuis," New York: Carroll & Graf Publishers, Inc., 1998

Schaefer, Richard T., "Race and Ethnicity in the United States," New York: HarperCollins College Publishers, 1995

Saunders, Gail, "Slavery in the Bahamas: 1648-1838," Nassau, Bahamas: The Nassau Guardian, 1985

Schaefer, Richard T., Racial and Ethnic Groups," Upper Saddle River, NJ: Prentice Hall, 2000

Schulke, Flip and McPhee, "King Remembered," New York: Pocket Books, 1986

Sharp, Saundra, "Black Women For Beginners, "New York: Writers and Readers Publishing, Incorporated, 1993

Smith, Elbert B., "The Death of Slavery: The United States, 1837-65," Chicago: The University of Chicago Press, 1967

Smith, Huston, "World's Religions, A Guide to Our Wisdom Traditions," San Francisco: HarperCollins, 1994

Smith, Huston, "The Soul of Christianity: Restoring the Great Tradition," San Francisco: HarperCollins, 2005

Smith, J. Alfred, "On The Jericho Road," Downers Grove, IL: InterVarsity Press, 2004

Smitherman, Geneva, "Talkin and Testifyin: The Language of Black Africans," Detroit: Wayne State University, 1985

Stein, Judith, "The World of Marcus Garvey," Baton Rouge, LA: Louisiana State University Press, 1986

Stevens, Peter F., "The Mayflower Murderer & Other Forgotten Firsts in American History," New York: William Morrow & Company, 1993

Stewart, Jeffrey C., "1001 Things Everyone Should Know About African American History," New York: Doubleday Main Street Books, 1996

Thorndike, E.L. and Barnhart, Clarence L., "Thorndike-Barnhart Student Dictionary, "Glenview, Ill: Scott Foresman, 1997

Turner, Johnathon et al., "Oppression: A Socio-History of Black-White Relations in America," Chicago: Nelson-Hall, 1984

Van Sertima, Ivan, "African Presence in Early America," New Brunswick, NJ: Rutgers University Press, 1987

Van Sertima, Ivan, "Great Black Leaders," New Brunswick, NJ: Rutgers University Press, 1988

Walker, Alice, "Langston Hughes: American Poet," San Francisco: Amistad/HarperCollins, 2002

Walker, Margaret, "Jubilee," Boston: Houghton Mifflin, 1966

Walter, Mildred P., "Kwanzaa, A Family Affair," New York: Avon Books, 1995

Walters, Raymond, "Du Bois and His Rivals," Columbia, MO: University of Missouri Press, 2002

Washington, Booker T., "Up From Slavery," New York: Oxford University Press, 1995

Washington, James M., "A Testament of Hope: The Essential Writings of

Martin Luther King, Jr.," San Francisco: Harper & Row Publishers, 1986

Washington, Joseph R., "Black Sects and Cults," Garden City, NY: Anchor Press/Doubleday, 1973

West, Cornell, "Race Matters," Boston: Beacon Press, 1993

Williams, Louis N., "Black Psychology," Washington, DC: University Press of America, Inc., 1981

Wilson, Ellen G., "The Loyal Blacks," New York: Capricorn Books, 1976

Wright, Donald R., "African Americans in the Colonial Era: From African Origins Through the American Revolution," Arlington Heights, IL: Harlan Davidson, Inc., 1990

Wright, Richard, "White Man, Listen!," New York: HarperCollins, 1995

Zack, Naomi, "American Mixed Race: The Culture of Microdiversity," New York: University Press of America, 1995

Zinn, Howard, "A People's History of the United States, 1492-Present," New York: Harper Perennial, 1995

Zirin, Dave, "What's My Name, Fool? Sports and Resistance in the United States," New York: Haymarket Books, 2005

PERIODICALS:

American Visions
Black Collegiate
Black Enterprise
Ebony
Essence
Emerge
Jet

JOURNALS:

Black Issues in Higher Education
Black Politics
Black Scholar
Journal of African American History
Journal of Negro History
Negro History Bulletin

INTERNET:

Black Issues in Higher Education (www.blackissues.com)
The Black World Today (www.tbwt.com.)
The Journal of Blacks in Higher Education (www.jbhe.com)

VIDEOS:

"America's Black Warriors: Two Wars To Win," A&E Television Networks. Cat. No. AAE-40352
"In the Words of Frederick Douglass," Tony Brown's Journal, #2201
"The Shackled Immigrants," Tony Brown's Journal, #2203
"Legends of Comedy," Tony Brown's Journal, #2206
"Black Communities After the Civil War," Films for the Humanities and Sciences, DAL8346
"Flight To Freedom: The Underground Railroad," Films for the Humanities and Sciences, DAL5864
"Great Black Women," Films for the Humanities and Sciences, DAL2308
"Reaching the Finish Line: Black Athletes and Civil Rights," Films for the Humanities and Sciences, DAL9204
"Understanding Race," Film for the Humanities, DAL8898

ABOUT THE AUTHORS & ILLUSTRATOR

MILTON COMBS, SR., M.A., M.Div., R.S.T.C.
He is now retired after nearly 30 years at Solano Community College in Northern California, where he developed and taught courses in African American studies, Ethnic Studies, and World Religions.

Grateful for the challenging and rewarding career he has had as a teacher, ordained minister, and overseas missionary, he is pleased to finally have time to pursue some of his book writing ideas. He has yet to write about the interesting and unique experiences he and his wife, Edna, and their four children had while living in Myanmar (Burma) from 1957-62. They were the first African American family to be commissioned by the American Baptist Foreign Mission Society to serve there.

Besides teaching, part of his background and experience has come from coordinating seminars and in-service training programs that focused on topics such as curriculum development, cultural diversity, church ministry, community youth programs, and establishing African American history organizations.

Macalester College, his alma mater, honored him with its Distinguished Citizen Alumni award in 1987, and Solano College selected him as one of its Distinguished Faculty in 1990. He has received numerous other awards for his contributions to education, the community, and the church. However, he says that this highest honor now is to co-author *The African American Quiz Book* with his daughter, Karyn.

As a member of Alpha Phi Alpha fraternity, the NAACP, and a number of other organizations, and a World War II veteran, he remains committed to his lifelong motto: "Be a doer of the Word, and not a hearer only."

KARYN COMBS, M.S., Ed.D.
She is the principal of Cherokee Elementary School on Eglin Air Force Base in Florida. In 2000, 2003, 2004, and 2005, the school achieved an "A+" rating according to the Department of Education and the School District of Okaloosa County based on the Florida Sunshine State Standards.

Dr. Karyn M. Combs also holds the rank of Master Sergeant as an Air Force Reservist with more than 20 years of service at Duke Field, 919th Special Operations

Wing, an auxiliary of Eglin AFB, FL. In this position, she has been a facilitator for the Non-Commissioned Officer Leadership Development Program (NCOLDP) and an instructor and advisor for the Military Equal Opportunity Program. She's had to travel to numerous Air Force Bases throughout the country to carry out these responsibilities. Recently, she received the "MEO Individual Award" at Duke Field for excellence in Military Equal Opportunity and leadership.

As an active participant in her community, she is a member of the Fort Walton Beach Charter Chapter of the American Business Women's Association (ABWA), Delta Sigma Theta Sorority, Inc., Okaloosa County Alumnae Chapter, Okaloosa County Branch, NAACP, Pensacola Chapter of the Links Inc., Blacks in Government (BIG) and Beulah First Baptist Church in Fort Walton Beach, Florida.

She has received many awards and honors from these organizations for her dedicated leadership and enthusiastic support of their programs. At the 2004 ABWA National Convention in Richmond, VA in October, she was selected ABWA's 2005 Business Woman of the Year for the United States. She is also a popular and much sought after motivation speaker. Her motto is: "Have faith in yourself and God and strive for excellence in all that you do."

J.D. COMPTON, illustrator

J.D. was given the gifts of the arts at the age of six. He deeply appreciates that his family, church, mentors and friends have all helped groom his various artistic talents. At the young age of 23 art, music, and dance are very important expressions in his busy life. His illustrations are shown in galleries, his Christian religious music is on CDs and choreographed for church dance, and he currently drums at an international worship center. The illustrations he has created for *The African American Quiz Book* greatly enhance its content.